W9-BMP-905

CULTURES OF THE WORLD®

ZIMBABWE

Sean Sheehan

NOT FOR SALE

BENCHMARK BOOKS

MARSHALL CAVENDISH
NEW YORK

PICTURE CREDITS
Cover photo: © Ian Murphy / Getty Images
AFP: 127 • Art Directors & Trip: 1, 5, 6, 18, 38, 46, 48, 50, 51, 52, 55, 64, 80, 92 • Bes Stock:
9 • Camera Press: 109, 122 • The Hutchison Library: 32, 36, 83, 89, 110, 112, 116 • The Image
Bank: 7, 60 • Interfoto: 25 • David Keith Jones / Images of Africa: 14 (bottom), 16, 102, 103
• Ann Jousiffe: 3, 4, 10, 12, 13, 14 (top), 39, 42, 61, 63, 66, 70, 72, 75, 95, 101, 105, 117, 123,
124, 126 • Life File: 8, 19, 41, 43, 45, 47, 69, 87, 113, 125 • Marshall Cavendish International
(Asia) Private Limited: 130, 131 • Ian Murphy: 40, 115 • National Archives of Zimbabwe:
23, 24, 26, 27, 29, 82, 84, 90, 107, 108, 119, 128 • Liba Taylor: 11, 15, 17, 20, 37, 44, 56, 57,
58, 62, 65, 68, 74, 76, 79, 88, 93, 97, 99, 111, 118, 121 • Travel Ink / Tim Lynch: 100 • UPI
/ Bettman: 30, 35

ACKNOWLEDGMENTS
Thanks to Barbara B. Brown, African Studies Center, Boston University,
for her expert reading of this manuscript

PRECEDING PAGE
Zimbabwean boys relax on a Morris Minor in Bulawayo.

Marshall Cavendish
99 White Plains Road
Tarrytown, NY 10591
Website: www.marshallcavendish.us

© Times Editions Pte Ltd 1996, 1993
© Marshall Cavendish International (Asia) Private Limited 2004
All rights reserved. First edition 1993. Second edition 2004.

® "Cultures of the World" is a registered trademark of Marshall Cavendish Corporation.

Originated and designed by Times Books International
An imprint of Marshall Cavendish International (Asia) Private Limited
A member of the Times Publishing Group

Library of Congress Cataloging-in-Publication Data
Sheehan, Sean, 1951-
Zimbabwe / by Sean Sheehan.— 2nd ed.
  p. cm. — (Cultures of the world)
Includes bibliographical references and index.
Contents: Geography — History — Government — Economy — Environment — Zimbabweans
— Lifestyle — Religion — Language — Arts — Leisure — Festivals — Foods.
ISBN 0-7614-1706-0
1. Zimbabwe—Juvenile literature. [1. Zimbabwe.] I. Title. II. Series: Cultures of the world
(2nd ed.)
DT2889.S54 2004
968.91—dc22   2003020883

Printed in China

7 6 5 4 3 2

CONTENTS

A cheetah waits for its prey in the plains of Zimbabwe. The fastest short-distance runner in the world, the cheetah can reach speeds of at least 60 miles (96 km) an hour.

A traditional village house in Zimbabwe is decorated with geometric patterns.

INTRODUCTION

FORMERLY KNOWN AS RHODESIA, the modern state of Zimbabwe evokes wonder. Gold hunters have looked for the Biblical King Solomon's mines in Zimbabwe. Historians and archeologists explore the nation's ancient sites to uncover clues about early humans. Nature lovers admire Zimbabwe's awesome wildlife, including one of the largest wild elephant populations in the world.

Political, economic, and social problems have put modern Zimbabwe in news headlines around the world. Zimbabwe's struggles to gain independence from Britain, establish a democratic government, and redistribute land have been accompanied by conflicts among the country's factions and ethnic groups.

Despite these problems, Zimbabwe remains one of the leading states of Africa. In their attempts to find a way to live and work together as fellow citizens, Zimbabweans have developed a unique culture and way of life.

GEOGRAPHY

ZIMBABWE IS SITUATED in the south of the African continent. Covering 150,873 square miles (390,761 square km), Zimbabwe is about the size of California. It is bounded on all sides by land: South Africa to the south, Botswana to the southwest, Zambia to the north, and Mozambique to the east, separating Zimbabwe from the Indian Ocean. Zimbabwe is blessed with natural resources that once helped make the nation one of Africa's most prosperous.

Opposite: **A village in the Matopo Hills region.**

Below: **Undulating terrain in the High Veld, a broad ridge that covers about a fourth of the country.**

THE SHAPE OF ZIMBABWE

Much of Zimbabwe is part of the great plateau dominating southern Africa. Shaped like a vast upside-down saucer, the plateau tilts upward toward the east, with areas of varying altitudes.

A high area known as the High Veld takes the form of a ridge that runs from the southwest to the northeast. This is the backbone of the country. Altitudes in this area do not fall below 4,000 feet (1,220 m) above sea level, making it ideal for cash-crop cultivation.

On each side of the High Veld lies the wider plateau of the Middle

Veld, with an elevation between 2,000 and 4,000 feet (610 and 1,220 m). Toward the south the Low Veld rises 500 to 2,000 feet (150 to 610 m). It is hot and dry, a poor place for cultivation.

THE MATOPO HILLS

The Matopo Hills are located 310 miles (500 km) south of Victoria Falls, near the city of Bulawayo. The hills, formed of granite and gneiss, are known as kopjes and are millions of years old. Caves there were home to the earliest human inhabitants of Zimbabwe. On the walls of the caves are paintings that date back some 2,000 years.

In the first half of the 19th century the Ndebele migrated to the Matopo Hills from their Zulu homelands. The Ndebele regarded the hills and caves of the Matopo region as sacred. When their king Mzilikazi died, his remains were sealed in a hillside tomb. The Ndebele still hold spiritual ceremonies in the Matopo Hills. The area is also the burial site of Cecil John Rhodes, the leader and financier of the first white settlers of Zimbabwe.

Geographically the Matopo Hills are interesting for the unusual granite outcrops that characterize the area. Wind and water have eroded and shaped the isolated granite blocks into strange and wonderful formations that resemble animals and human faces. Some of the rocks are precariously balanced one on top of the other, while others lie scattered as if they had been thrown around by a mighty giant. Mzilikazi named the area Matobos, meaning the baldheaded ones, after the granite masses; the word was later corrupted to Matopos.

ROCK FORMATIONS The undulating landscape of the High Veld is interrupted by intrusions of hard rock. A notable example of these formations is the Great Dike, 300 miles (480 km) long, 6 miles (10 km) wide. Formed by solidified magma resulting from volcanic activity millions of years ago, the Great Dike contains rich seams of chromite, asbestos, nickel, and platinum. Its mineral-rich content is one of the country's most valuable resources.

The Matopo Hills are another example of formations caused by these intrusions. However, the Matopo Hills are dwarfed by the mountainous Eastern Highlands, where Inyangani, at 8,560 feet (2,608 m), rises as the highest mountain in Zimbabwe.

RIVERS

There are two main rivers in Zimbabwe: the Limpopo in the south and the Zambezi in the north. Both help to define the country's political borders. The Limpopo separates Zimbabwe from the Republic of South Africa, while the Zambezi marks the boundary with Zambia.

ZAMBEZI The Zambezi flows for 1,650 miles (2,655 km), making it one of the longest rivers in Africa. After the Zambezi's dramatic 300-foot (90-m) drop into a mile-wide chasm at Victoria Falls, the river flows through the Kariba Gorge. There its waters are harnessed by a dam, forming the 2,000-square mile (5,180-square km) Lake Kariba. The enormous mass of water creates great pressure and feeds a power station that supplies electricity to Zimbabwe and Zambia.

Left: **A bridge over the Zambezi River.**

Opposite: **Balancing rocks of granite and gneiss are a notable feature of the Matopo landscape.**

Lake Kariba, the largest artificial lake in the world after Egypt's Lake Nasser, was formed by the damming of the Zambezi River. Many river dwellers had to be resettled when the lake was created, and countless animals had to be rescued when their habitats were flooded. Today animal and bird life flourishes on the shores of the lake.

LIMPOPO The Limpopo is 1,100 miles (1,770 km) long and flows north from South Africa, forming that country's borders with Botswana and Zimbabwe. Changes in the volume of the river affect people in nearby areas. A drought may dry up the river basin and reduce the water supply, while a cyclone may cause the basin to flood some areas.

Until tensions between South Africa and Zimbabwe relaxed in the 1990s, the section of the Limpopo between the two countries was filled with steel netting. This was to catch the floating mines that South Africa feared would be released by black nationalist guerillas operating from Zimbabwe. The section of the river is still heavily guarded, though now it is to prevent jobless Zimbabweans from crossing into South Africa to work there.

VICTORIA FALLS

Victoria Falls, situated on the Zambezi River, is described as one of the seven natural wonders of the world. More than 150 million years old, the falls were created at a time when volcanic lava from the earth's crust cooled and contracted, forming crevices. These crevices gradually expanded under the influence of the flooding of the Zambezi, resulting in a gorge. The gorge now receives a vast cascade of water from the Zambezi River as it tumbles into the chasm.

The tremendous power of the water falling 355 feet (108 m) creates a terrific roar that can be heard from a distance of 25 miles (40 km). In addition to the noise, clouds of spray rise into the air and create a mist that is visible nearly 4 miles (6.5 km) away. The African name for the falls is Mosi-oa-tunya, which means the smoke that thunders.

David Livingstone, the 19th-century Scottish explorer and missionary, is often referred to as the person who discovered Victoria Falls. Livingstone first saw the falls in 1855 and named them in honor of Britain's Queen Victoria.

It is more accurate to credit Livingstone with being the first white person to see the falls, as he had been taken there by local Africans to view the spectacle. Livingstone's astonishment at the phenomenon, as he traveled along the Zambezi River, is recorded in his diary. He described the falls as being so impressive that they "must have been gazed on by angels in their flight."

CLIMATE

Zimbabwe's climate varies by altitude, with the low-lying areas being the hottest. October is the warmest month, when average temperature highs reach 86°F (30°C) on the Low Veld and 72°F (22°C) on the High Veld. The summer season lasts from September to April. Wintertime, from May to August, is coldest on the High Veld. Although the nights are cold, the days are usually warm and sunny.

Bamboo thrives along river banks.

The cooler temperatures on the High Veld, combined with regular rainfall, help produce an ideal climate for farming. The subtropical conditions provide a perfect environment for grass to grow tall and for raising cattle. The main towns in the High Veld, Harare and Bulawayo, receive an average of eight hours of sunshine every day throughout the year.

Rainfall is heaviest in the Eastern Highlands, where the monsoon winds cross from the Indian Ocean to meet the tall mountains. The winds are forced high into the sky, where they form heavy clouds of water droplets. The consequent rains help to water this part of the country, resulting in lush vegetation.

In the low-lying areas, the climate is dry and hot and not conducive to farming. The grass is coarse, and only bush and thorny trees manage to prosper in the harsh and dry heat. The lack of rainfall means that growing crops on a commercial basis is often unprofitable. Nevertheless, there has been success in irrigating the Low Veld in the southeast. Land that was once suitable only for ranching is proving to be lucrative agriculturally.

VEGETATION

Much of Zimbabwe's terrain consists of grassland. There are evergreen forests in the east and savanna woodland in the west. Brachystegia, a tall hardwood, grows in the Middle Veld and the High Veld.

Many of Zimbabwe's most beautiful wildflowers grow in the Nyanga region in the Eastern Highlands. The flame lily, for example, the national flower of Zimbabwe, is a climbing vine with bright red flowers that bloom in summer.

One of the most famous trees in Zimbabwe, found in many parts of Africa, is the baobab tree. It grows in the drier areas of south and southwestern Zimbabwe. In times of drought, elephants eat the juicy wood beneath the bark of the baobab tree.

The baobab tree has a thick trunk and many branches that spread outward, sometimes with leaves, other times bare. Large white flowers bloom between October and December. The fiber of the bark of the tree can be used to make rope and cloth.

The baobab often lives for more than a thousand years. In the vicinity of Victoria Falls, there is a famous baobab tree that bears the signature of David Livingstone; it is reported to be more than a thousand years old.

The sausage tree, with its large gray-brown, sausage-shaped pods, is another interesting member of Zimbabwe's flora. The sausage fruit is inedible, but its leaves and deep red flowers are food for antelopes, baboons, bats, birds, and elephants.

The baobab tree grows in the valleys of the Zambezi and Limpopo rivers.

13

Antelopes and zebras in the plains of Zimbabwe.

FAUNA

A great diversity of animals lives in the wild and in parks and reserves in Zimbabwe. Elephants, hippopotamuses, and crocodiles abound. Lions and giraffes are also common.

Antelopes and zebras are favorite targets for hungry lions, although antelopes can often outrun a lion during a chase and zebras can deliver a fatal kick when attacked.

Aardvarks and zorillas, though far apart in the dictionary, live side by side in Zimbabwe. The aardvark eats insects. It uses its long and narrow snout to forage close to the ground and its donkey-like ears to detect sounds of danger. Like the aardvark, the zorilla, or African polecat, is a nocturnal creature. Its diet, however, is more varied. It feeds on small mammals, birds, and invertebrates. Like skunks, zorillas excrete a foul smell to repel predators.

Zimbabwe's venomous snakes include boomslangs, black-necked cobras, and mambas. The mamba is one of the world's most venomous

HWANGE NATIONAL PARK

The largest national park in Zimbabwe is Hwange, covering nearly 6,000 square miles (15,540 square km) in the northwestern corner of the country. The next most important park is Mana Pools, some 248 miles (400 km) north of the capital, Harare, where the increasingly rare black rhinoceros is found.

The Hwange National Park is home to about 20,000 elephants, and the number is growing at a rate of 5 percent a year. There are also other animals, including 413 species of birds. The land itself forms the most easterly side of the vast Kalahari Desert that covers two-thirds of neighboring Botswana. The national park was formed in 1929 because no other use for the land could be found. Parts of it had formerly been a Ndebele hunting reserve. Today the only hunters are tourists who take part in controlled safari hunts. Quotas for trophy animals are set by a government department. Between August and October, visitors flock to Hwange National Park to watch the animals.

snakes. There are four species: three green and one black. The black mamba moves very fast and will chase its prey before injecting it with a powerful nerve toxin. The green mambas are not as aggressive as the black species and will not usually attack mammals. They prefer lizards, eggs, and small birds.

ANTELOPES Zimbabwe is home to many species of antelopes, such as the impala, with its patches of black fur above its hoofs. The males have gently spiraling horns. The gnu, or wildebeest, travels in groups varying in size from a dozen to a few hundred.

The kudu has light stripes and stands about 4 feet (1.2 m) tall at the shoulder. The male has long corkscrew-like horns that can grow as long as 3 feet (0.9 m).

Klipspringers feed in family groups and warn one another with a shrill whistle if they sense a predator.

NATURAL LANDSCAPES

Apart from the highlands in the eastern part of the country, most of Zimbabwe is generally flat. The highest mountain in the country is Inyangani, at 8,504 feet (2,592 m), while the lowest point is found in the south of the country where the Rundi and Save rivers meet at an altitude of 531 feet (162 m) above sea level.

The scenery changes from one area to the next. A drive across the country passes through a variety of natural landscapes such as plains, mountains, valleys, and forests.

In the Eastern Highlands, the mountains and valleys have an Alpine look, but the names of the ranges are unmistakably African: Inyanga, Umvukwe, Chimanimani. Once a refuge for people fleeing danger, the highlands now attract vacationers seeking outdoor leisure pursuits such as fishing, hiking, and climbing.

TOWNSCAPES

Zimbabwe's cities, towns, and villages are remarkably tidy and well-groomed. Streets in downtown areas are usually wide, a legacy of the days when they were planned to enable an ox-and-wagon team to turn around. Trees and colorful flowers line the roads, and the towns' names are planted in foxgloves and marigolds in local parks.

HARARE The capital of Zimbabwe was founded in 1890. Originally Salisbury, the capital's name was changed to Harare when Zimbabwe became independent in 1980.

Harare's population has exceeded 1.8 million and is still growing as more people migrate from the countryside to find employment there. However, there are not enough jobs for everyone, and the poor live in

shanty dwellings. The broad streets of Harare are characteristic of most Zimbabwean towns. Because of the pleasant climate year-round, parks and open spaces are filled with flowers. Even the trees bordering the streets flower in the summer.

BULAWAYO The second largest city in Zimbabwe, Bulawayo, has a population of nearly 930,000. It is an important industrial center; the surrounding area is rich in mineral deposits, and there are a number of large mines.

The city also attracts a large number of tourists because of its transportation links with Victoria Falls and the national parks. Bulawayo has historical importance; it was the center of what was once called Matabeleland—homeland to the Ndebele people, the most significant ethnic group in Zimbabwe after the Shona people.

CHITUNGWIZA This city in the northeast was formed in 1978 out of a group of small settlements. It has grown into the third largest city in Zimbabwe and is home to close to 400,000 people. Not many of the residents of Chitungwiza work there; most of them travel to the capital, 15 miles (25 km) north, for work.

Situated at an altitude of 4,865 feet (1,482 m), Harare has a temperate climate.

HISTORY

EVIDENCE OF A DISTINCTIVE Stone Age culture in Zimbabwe goes back 500,000 years. The early peoples were hunters and gatherers. They later settled down in agricultural communities.

The earliest non-Africans to arrive in the land between the Limpopo and Zambezi rivers were Muslim traders, who were active on the eastern coast from the 10th century. After the Arabs came the Portuguese, but it was the British in the 19th century who made a permanent impression. They expropriated the land and named it Rhodesia.

Only after years of violent struggle did the country return to African rule. In 1980 Rhodesia was renamed Zimbabwe, after the ancient ruins, found about 17 miles (27 km) outside Masvingo (formerly Fort Victoria).

EARLY HISTORY

Most scholars believe that Africa was the birthplace of the human race. Stone tools and weapons such as hammers and spearheads have been discovered in Africa that date back some 2 million years. Early people in Zimbabwe also used the pigments from the iron in basalt rock to paint pictures, in shades of yellow, red, and brown, in caves. These ancient paintings are still well preserved.

It is thought that the San, or Bushmen, who still live in the Kalahari Desert of South Africa, are the descendants of the original inhabitants of southern and central Africa. The early San were driven into the desert by Bantu-speaking peoples when they migrated to this region.

Above: **An ancient painting of antelopes in a cave at Matopos, home to the San more than 2,000 years ago.**

Opposite: **A passageway in the ruins at Great Zimbabwe, which was once a thriving center of trade and commerce.**

The ruins of the Great Enclosure, part of Great Zimbabwe, whose stone structures were built without cement.

GREAT ZIMBABWE

Archeological evidence dates the arrival of an early Bantu culture in Zimbabwe around A.D. 300. The imposing stone structures of Great Zimbabwe were built by a Bantu-speaking people known as Shona, between the 12th and 15th centuries.

The structures make up three sections: the Hill Complex, the Valley Complex, and the Great Enclosure. They are the largest and most important constructions made by humans in southern Africa before modern times. Early settlers from the West thought that the structures had been built by the ancient Egyptians or Phoenicians rather than by Africans in the area.

The Shona word *zimbabwe* translates as royal court. More than 200 stone structures were erected as the residences and power bases of the local kings and their representatives.

The Hill Complex is a steep 330 foot-high (100 m-high) granite hill dotted with ruins. A walled space near the summit may have been the king's headquarters or the seat of a royal spirit medium. The space contained stone bird figures, which were plundered by Europeans at the end of the 19th century. The Shona believed that the spiritual advisers to the king could communicate with their ancestors through the cries of the birds represented by the stone figures.

The Great Enclosure is a massive elliptical structure 30 feet (9 m) in height and 800 feet (244 m) in circumference. Thought to be the king's palace, the Great Enclosure contains a conical tower, the purpose and meaning of which remain unknown.

The Valley Complex has several ruins, indicating that the area was the social and political capital of Zimbabwe during the 14th and 15th centuries. Evidence of gold smelting and an elaborate drainage system point to a prosperous community, which had a sophisticated trading network. Gold and copper from more than a thousand mines were exported through Mozambique to the coast to be shipped across the Indian Ocean. Manufactured goods were imported.

Centuries later, gold was found in some of Great Zimbabwe's ruins. A group of early European looters even founded a company called the Rhodesian Ancient Ruins Company.

Today Great Zimbabwe remains remarkable and impressive. It is the country's most popular tourist attraction after Victoria Falls. The ruins are the remains of a medieval African civilization that had a capital city of 10,000 people and that extended over most of what is Zimbabwe today.

LOBENGULA

In the 19th century, whenever foreigners wanted to mine for gold in Zimbabwe, they went to Lobengula, the undisputed king of the land. Lobengula was no fool. He saw the greed of the white entrepreneurs who were so interested in his kingdom and did his best to contain their ambitions.

In 1888 Cecil Rhodes managed to secure an exclusive treaty with Lobengula through John Moffat, the son of the famous missionary Robert Moffat. In the early stages of negotiations, Lobengula was under the impression that no more than 10 Europeans would mine in his land at any time and that they would be subject to the law and authority of the Ndebele people.

However, the conditions that Lobengula expected never found their way onto paper, and Lobengula unknowingly signed away some of his people's valuable rights. He was tricked into granting a concession allowing the Europeans access to all the minerals in the "kingdom, principalities and domains, together with full power to do all things that they may deem necessary to win and procure same."

When Lobengula found out exactly what he had agreed to, he tried to cancel the agreement, but it was too late. Rhodes had persuaded the British government to give the British South Africa Company the right to enter the country and undertake business there. By 1900 the British South Africa Company had established complete control in the new territory.

After three years, it was clear that the foreigners intended to make Ndebele land their home. Lobengula came under pressure from his own people to fight. He knew that his people's spears were no match for the guns of the Europeans, but Lobengula had to enter into battle to protect his people's land.

Soon the Ndebele were forced to set Bulawayo on fire and flee. Lobengula died some time later, a very disillusioned king.

CECIL RHODES

For nearly a century, Zimbabwe was known to the world as Rhodesia, after Cecil Rhodes, an Englishman who worked with great zeal to bring to the Africans what he believed to be the greatest civilization on Earth. His ambition was to paint the map red—it was the practice of mapmakers to mark in red parts of the world that were part of the British empire. He also wanted to build a railroad from the tip of South Africa to northern Egypt.

At age 17 Rhodes left his home in England to join his brother on a cotton farm in Natal, South Africa. He later made his fortune by buying the rights to diamond fields in Kimberly. In a few years, he had amassed the rights to 90 percent of the world's diamonds.

Hearing the tales of adventurers about large reserves of gold in the land across the Limpopo River, Rhodes then set his sights on Zimbabwe. In 1890 he organized a group of 200 men who crossed the Limpopo and claimed the land that became Fort Victoria. His actions were justified on the grounds of the Rudd concession, negotiated with Lobengula, giving the British South Africa Company the right to mine in this area.

Rhodes's name lives on, no longer in the name of a country, but in the scholarships he established at Oxford University.

Cecil Rhodes was a leading proponent of British colonialism in Africa in the late 19th century.

THE SEEDS OF REVOLUTION

The British South Africa Company ran Rhodesia until the 1920s. In 1923 Rhodesia became Southern Rhodesia, a self-governing colony of the British empire. This made no difference to most Africans, since the right to vote was based on British citizenship.

The traditional communal farming economy of the Africans was destroyed when the Europeans began amassing large tracts of land for their farms. Dispossessed Africans were employed as cheap labor or left to try to farm infertile land. Africans could not change their place of work without permission from their employers, and laws requiring Africans to carry passes made it easy to control the local population.

After World War II, large numbers of Europeans were attracted to Zimbabwe by the idea of making a prosperous living out of farming. The situation for the Africans deteriorated as the European population increased. New laws further dispossessed the African population of their ancestors' land.

WORKING IN THE MINES

When the European prospectors realized that Rhodesia's gold reserves were not as rich as they had imagined, they hired African miners at very low wages in order to make a profit. The Africans endured forced labor in the mines, and many died. The workers christened the mines with names indicating clearly how they felt about the experience:

- Makombera (makh-ohm-BERH-rah)—you are closed in
- Maplanki (mah-PLAHN-ki)—planks for punishment
- Mtshalwana (mit-shahl-WAH-NA)—you will fight one another
- Sigebengu (sig-erh-BENG-OO)—bosses are villains

The years after World War II saw the growth of nationalist aspirations, not only in Rhodesia but all across Africa. Despite strong opposition from nationalists, in 1953 a federation was formed between Southern Rhodesia (Zimbabwe), Northern Rhodesia (Zambia), and Nyasaland (Malawi). In 1963 the federation was dissolved, with Northern Rhodesia and Nyasaland only months from independence. In Southern Rhodesia, however, the European population dug their heels in, resisting calls for liberalization.

AFRICAN NATIONALISM

African nationalism in Southern Rhodesia made itself felt in the 1950s when a bus boycott against fare increases was organized in the capitol. In 1957 the African National Congress (ANC) was formed, calling for "the national unity of all inhabitants of this country in true partnership regardless of race, color, and creed." People held strikes and marches, leading to a ban on the ANC.

The repression intensified the fight for independence from minority rule. Opposition spread across the cities, and the army responded to a strike in Bulawayo by killing 18 demonstrators.

In 1961 the Zimbabwe African People's Union (ZAPU) was formed. Joshua Nkomo became its leader. A couple of years later, the Zimbabwe African National Union (ZANU) was formed. A leading member of ZANU was Robert Mugabe.

Joshua Nkomo, leader of ZAPU, inspecting his forces.

The Unilateral Declaration of Independence (UDI) was signed by Ian Smith on November 11, 1965.

UNILATERAL DECLARATION OF INDEPENDENCE

As many parts of Africa gained independence from colonial rule, the British rulers became alarmed at the prospect of losing their power and privileges in Rhodesia. In 1965, after inconclusive discussions with the British government over African rule in Rhodesia, the Rhodesian prime minister, Ian Douglas Smith, signed a Unilateral Declaration of Independence announcing the country's refusal to be bound by Britain.

The declaration stated, without agreement from Britain, that from November 11, 1965, the day the declaration was signed, Rhodesia would have complete authority over its own affairs. Britain did not recognize the declaration and stopped all trade with Rhodesia. The next year, the United Nations imposed economic sanctions on Rhodesia.

Amid problems arising from international sanctions and African nationalism, in 1970 the white minority government declared Rhodesia a republic. Britain and other countries did not recognize the government and constitution of the Rhodesian republic.

At the same time, the black majority was not happy about being governed by the white minority. Nationalist sentiments grew stronger, and in 1972 the Second Chimurenga broke out. Nationalist guerrillas trained in Zambia fought to liberate the country from white dominance. Numerous attacks were launched on Rhodesian security forces. As the guerrillas won the respect and understanding of the rural communities, government forces found it difficult to suppress the armed resistance.

Finally, in 1980, the Lancaster House Agreement led to the start of Rhodesia's transition from a British colony to the independent nation of Zimbabwe. A new prime minister, Robert Mugabe, was elected, and a new constitution was approved.

"I don't believe in majority rule ever in Rhodesia, not in a thousand years."

—Ian Smith, 1976

TIME FOR CHANGE

Despite popular discontent over the uneven distribution of land—with the white minority owning most of it—and government corruption, Mugabe continued to win elections throughout the 1980s and 1990s. In 1987 he became president, and his party, ZANU, merged with Joshua Nkomo's ZAPU opposition party to form the Zimbabwe African National Union Patriotic Front (ZANU-PF).

In the late 1990s, amid growing economic problems, people began protesting the high tax rates and veterans of the war for independence demanded compensation. In 1998, despite international opposition, the Mugabe government seized white-owned farms and gave the land to the war veterans. This also caused disruptions to agricultural work and worsened economic problems in the country.

As Zimbabwe dealt with high inflation rates and food shortages, opposition toward Mugabe's leadership intensified. In 1999 a new opposition party, the Movement for Democratic Change (MDC), posed a serious threat to ZANU-PF. Although the MDC performed well at the elections, Mugabe managed to hold on to power. In 2003 there was widespread evidence of electoral fraud.

GOVERNMENT

IN THE EARLY YEARS after independence from white-minority rule, nearly a quarter of the white population fled, fearing an impending dictatorship. A fairly democratic state emerged instead, but in the 1990s, as Mugabe's determination to hold on to power at all costs became increasingly obvious, fears of a dictatorship materialized among many of Zimbabwe's black citizens as well.

In 1999 opposition groups began campaigning for changes in the country's constitution that would strengthen democratic rule. Mugabe, however, wanted to change the constitution to strengthen his political control. At the same time, the Movement for Democratic Change (MDC) emerged as the voice of opposition to ZANU-PF.

In 2000, when Mugabe lost a referendum, some 55 percent of the electorate voted to reject the government's revised constitution. The people campaigned for a constitutional change to limit the president's powers and time in office. The Mugabe government amended the constitution to legitimize the seizure of white-owned farms.

Mugabe's efforts to stay in power have included opposition bullying and vote rigging. The MDC party has won a number of by-elections, in which it has faced violent opposition from government supporters. Foreign journalists have also been expelled for reporting on illegal activities by the Mugabe government.

A new constitution is likely to emerge, but not before the country achieves some balance in political and economic power. The land issue lies behind much of the political wrangling in Zimbabwe's government. Until the land issue is resolved, it is unlikely that a new and lasting constitution will emerge. Countries such as South Africa have made attempts to mediate Zimbabwe's political and economic crisis. There has also been talk about an early retirement for Mugabe that would allow the country to move into a new era of government.

"There is a place for everyone in this country. We want to ensure a sense of security for both the winners and the losers."

—Robert Mugabe, 1980

Opposite: **The Parliament House in Harare, the capital and administrative center of Zimbabwe.**

DEMOCRACY OR DICTATORSHIP?

"The government has seriously failed and the people are now saying, 'Enough is enough!'"

—The MDC mayor of Harare, June 2003.

SIGNS OF DEMOCRACY For seven years, ZANU allowed 20 seats in the parliament for whites, when their minority status would hardly have justified more than one or two seats.

Zimbabwe is a one-party state, but opposition parties are allowed. The Movement for Democratic Change has contested elections, claiming that the elections were rigged.

Now that ZANU-PF has emerged as the only viable party, there is a likelihood that the use of powers such as the Emergency Powers Act will decrease.

Compared to the rest of Africa, Zimbabwe has a good record of constitutional rule. Signs of an independent press can be seen in the newspapers's allegations of government corruption. The University of Zimbabwe has also been a source of strident anti-government criticism. The university has been closed down from time to time because of this, but it continues to flourish.

SIGNS OF DICTATORSHIP ZANU-PF is committed to a one-party state, leaving no alternative for voters during elections. In the period of unrest following independence, there were serious allegations of mistreatment, and in some cases murder, of the Ndebele minority. The government does not allow organizations such as Amnesty International to investigate human rights violations in Zimbabwe. Television and radio are owned and controlled by the government.

The Emergency Powers Act gives the government the right to act in a way that is undemocratic in cases that it considers to be emergencies. When the former prime minister Abel Muzorewa spoke out against the ZANU government, he was jailed on charges of subversion.

Robert Mugabe, making a speech to the UN General Assembly on world environment and development.

ROBERT MUGABE

Robert Mugabe was imprisoned for 10 years by the white-minority government of the country in which he now serves as president. Born in 1922, he received six years' elementary education in a mission school. Later, he studied for two years to become a teacher. During his years in prison, he finished six college degrees.

HIS SUCCESSES Mugabe became the leader of ZANU because of his radical opposition to white-minority rule and his unwillingness to compromise on the issue of black-majority rule. He was portrayed in the media as a monster and the country's number-one public enemy. When ZANU won in the 1980 elections and Mugabe became the leader of the country, the black community celebrated in the streets although there was apprehension among the white population.

In time, Mugabe convinced the whites that they had nothing to fear and won their respect. But there was opposition from the Ndebele minority. It took nearly 10 years of bloodshed and the loss of countless lives for Mugabe to merge the Ndebele with the new Zimbabwe.

Mugabe supporters making their presence felt at a ZANU rally in Harare.

HIS FAILURES Although Mugabe won landslide election victories in the 1990s, his popularity soon began to decline very quickly. His failure to solve basic economic problems concerning economic growth and the creation of sustained employment resulted in bread riots and severe fuel shortages.

The land issue remains a controversial policy that has lost Zimbabwe a lot of international respect. International investors are dissuaded from investing in a country where the government seizes economic resources for political reasons.

Zimbabwe's political and economic situation in 2003 raised the probability that Mugabe would finally relinquish his grip on power after more than 20 years of rule, leaving the country to grapple with the question of whom to elect in his place and how to do so democratically.

THE OPPOSITION

The main opposition party to ZANU-PF is the multiethnic MDC. Despite

SYSTEM OF GOVERNMENT

In theory, Zimbabwe is a parliamentary democracy with a constitution guaranteeing individual freedom, regardless of race, religion, or gender. In practice, Zimbabwe is a dictatorship that abuses its constitution.

The parliament consists of a House of Assembly with 150 members. Constitutional changes are supposed to have the support of two-thirds of the members of the Assembly.

The most powerful political position is that of the president. There is no limit to the number of consecutive terms the president can serve.

putting up a good fight in national elections, the MDC party has not been able to topple the ZANU-PF party. Nevertheless, on the local level, the MDC party has had several victories. Zimbabwe has eight provinces (Manicaland, Mashonaland Central, Mashonaland East, Mashonaland West, Masvingo, Matabeleland North, Matabeleland South, and Midlands) and two cities recognized as provinces (Harare and Bulawayo). Each province is run by its own local government.

In the local government election in March 2002, the capital city of Harare voted overwhelmingly for the MDC party. As a result, the local government of Harare formed an MDC council and chose an MDC mayor, Elias

The government's concern for the welfare of its people is reflected in health projects that provide medical advice and assistance to those who need them.

Mudzuri. However, Mudzuri soon came into conflict with the national government, and in less than two months he was suspended by a ZANU-PF minister. The decision on whether the suspension was legal was left to the courts.

The conflict between Harare's mayor and the central government reflects the wider conflict between the MDC opposition party and the ZANU-PF ruling party on a national scale. In 2003 the MDC party called for peaceful protest marches to demonstrate the level of discontent among the people of Zimbabwe. Zimbabwe's prospects for a peaceful future depend partly on the intervention of other African leaders to promote a political settlement in the country.

ECONOMY

ZIMBABWE HAS A WEALTH of natural resources, with large deposits of valuable minerals lying near fertile agricultural lands. While the country usually produces enough agriculturally to feed itself, it still has major economic problems to deal with.

Blessed with a farm-friendly climate, Zimbabwean land is able to support a wide variety of crops. Wheat, barley, oats, millet, soybeans, and groundnuts are all produced on a commercial basis. Tobacco is the most valuable crop, although sugar, tea, and coffee are also important. There are also large farms devoted to raising livestock: cattle, pigs, and sheep.

The main economic problems in Zimbabwe stem from the poor distribution and use of fertile land. More than half of all Zimbabweans earn a living directly from agriculture, but less than 15 percent of the country's arable land is being cultivated, and people do not have equal access to the country's rich agricultural resources.

Unequal land ownership, a major concern of the government of independent Zimbabwe, is a legacy of the nation's colonial history. When the colonialists turned to agriculture to obtain profits, they took large tracts of land away from the local farmers, who were sent to remote areas where they had to work under harsh conditions in order to earn a meager living.

Most of the country's most fertile land today remains in the hands of a small section of the population—the big commercial farmers. Farming families in the rural areas cultivate the remaining, less fertile land. Their plots do not produce enough to support their families. Poverty affects a large section of the Zimbabwean population.

Above: **Agricultural land near Harare.**

Opposite: **A Zimbabwean buys a handmade basket at a street market.**

A white farmer on his farm. Many large farms in Zimbabwe use modern agricultural methods and equipment.

THE LEGACY OF RACISM

When Zimbabwe gained independence from Britain in 1980, a third of its arable land belonged to a white minority that made up just 1 percent of the population. The white farmers had tremendous economic power, because their land produced nearly half of the country's annual income in exports.

Mugabe and his party promised to resettle more than 150,000 black families on white-owned land. The government bought land from white farmers, but land reform proceded very slowly. In 1990 the government began taking over white-owned farms, compensating the owners with government bonds. That triggered international criticism and reduced foreign investment. Domestically, black farmers violently seized and occupied farms owned by whites.

The land issue remains unresolved. Thousands of black families have so far been resettled, but many Zimbabweans are still trying to make a living from land that was set aside for them by past white governments.

There is a pressing need to resettle them in areas better suited for cultivation. Their land is overpopulated and overcultivated, resulting in problems such as deforestation and soil erosion. Irregular rainfall can cause serious droughts, as in early 1992 when a drought reached crisis proportions. People's lives were at risk, and the country had to look to other countries for food supplies.

The ongoing crisis over the seizure of white-owned farms is adding to the country's economic woes. In 2001 the production of corn, the basic food crop, dropped by 25 percent.

TOBACCO FARMING

Tobacco is one of Zimbabwe's most valuable products. More than half a million people work on tobacco farms in the country. Tobacco is the country's biggest foreign currency earner.

Tobacco is Zimbabwe's most important crop.

Zimbabwean tobacco is of high quality. Most of it is exported to European countries. Production has been cut back slightly in favor of cotton and food crops such as sugar, wheat, and sorghum, but tobacco farming remains economically valuable.

On tobacco farms, seedlings are planted in November to catch the rainfall at that time of the year. The seedlings require plenty of water, but the soil must also be well-drained in order for for them to thrive.

There is a moral issue involved in the production of tobacco for the manufacture of cigarettes because of the harmful effects of smoking on health. One way Zimbabwe can respond to criticism about its social responsibility as a major global tobacco producer is to find other uses for tobacco that do not endanger the health of the consumer.

Some of Zimbabwe's largest commercial timber plantations are found in the Eastern Highlands.

RICH DIVERSITY

There is far more to Zimbabwe's agricultural economy than just tobacco farming. When the winter months in the Northern Hemisphere deprive Europeans of fresh flowers, Zimbabwe is happy to meet the demand, packing some 300 tons (272 metric tons) of fresh flowers for export every week.

Softwoods such as pine and eucalyptus are grown commercially, especially in the Eastern Highlands. Zimbabwe has some of the world's tallest eucalyptus trees, which originally came from Australia.

Tea is farmed intensively, and Zimbabwe is self-sufficient in the crop. Coffee plantations are on the increase. Hops are also grown to produce Zimbabwe's lager beer, which is exported to countries such as the United States. When other countries were imposing sanctions on white Rhodesia, some farmers established vineyards to meet the demand for wine in the absence of imports. Today Zimbabwe produces good-quality white wine.

Raising cattle for the export of beef was introduced by the white settlers. It remains an important part of the economy. To black farmers, cattle signify power and prestige, but they lack capital and good grazing land to raise cattle on a commercial scale.

INDUSTRY

Most of Zimbabwe's minerals are exported, while the rest provide the country with the raw materials for its industries. The Great Dike has reserves of platinum and chromite that will provide a secure future for mining in the country long after the reserves of copper and nickel have been depleted.

The Iron and Steel Corporation employs 6,000 people, making it one of the largest employers of industrial workers. The company produces a variety of metal products for use in manufacturing everything from plowshares to components for locomotive engines.

Zimbabwe's power industry includes the massive Kariba Dam, which it shares with Zambia, on the Zambezi River. The construction of new hydroelectric plants along Zimbabwe's rivers will add enormously to the country's ability to meet its energy needs.

Most of Zimbabwe's industry is located in the vicinity of the two main centers of population, Harare and Bulawayo. Both have vital railroad connections. In the eastern part of the country, where important timber plantations are located, the town of Mutare (moo-TAR-ay) is a hub of commercial activity, largely due to its strategic road link with the busy Mozambique port of Beira on the eastern coast of Africa.

The Kariba Dam provides hydroelectric power for industries and cities.

Zimbabwean miners take a break.

MINING

Mining is the oldest industry in Zimbabwe, dating back thousands of years to the Iron Age. Burial sites of Iron Age nobility that have been excavated reveal a sophisticated use of gold. Some of the finds include seashells set in gold and delicate necklaces of twisted gold. However, perhaps due to its abundance, gold was not worshiped as the ultimate mineral. Jewelry crafted from iron was just as highly regarded.

Nevertheless, it was gold that attracted the attention of the Arab traders, Portuguese navigators, and British entrepreneurs. The British thought that so many gold mines promised equally abundant profits, but many of the mines they tried to exploit had already been worked dry and the ones that were still mineworthy often did not repay the investment in machinery. Then a gold prospector discovered coal near Victoria Falls, and that started a profitable coal industry that is still important to Zimbabwe's economy.

Apart from gold and coal, Zimbabwe is also rich in other valuable minerals. In the 1950s emeralds were discovered, and 10 years later enormous nickel reserves. The 1970s brought a bigger surprise—the discovery of platinum. A modern plant opened in 1992, supplied by the world's largest reserve of platinum outside South Africa. Some 50 minerals, including chromium, cobalt, copper, iron, silver, and tin, are mined in Zimbabwe.

While many countries in Africa have become dependent on a core natural resource, such as oil in Nigeria or copper in Zambia, Zimbabwe relies on several, which makes it relatively resilient to fluctuations in commodity prices. For example, when the price of asbestos fell due to concerns about its effect on health and the environment, Zimbabwe did not suffer catastrophic consequences for its annual production.

A pottery workshop at the Mzilikazi Craft Center produces beautiful figures of animals, bowls, and plates to cater to a growing tourist industry.

ECONOMIC PROSPECTS

Zimbabwe's natural resources are a firm foundation for economic growth. However, growth hinges on a settlement of the country's political crisis. An urgent need is for the land issue to be resolved so that agricultural production can progress.

Forestry is a new economic resource that could become more profitable in the future. Large areas have been planted with softwoods that can be harvested for pulp. In the southwest of the country, there are new plantations of teak and mahogany.

A more controversial source of export income is the manufacture of ammunitions. Factories based in the capital, Harare, produce high-explosive shells and other weapons for export, mostly to other African countries.

Guests of the Holiday Inn in Harare enjoy a buffet in the hotel's dining area.

TOURISM

Tourism grew rapidly in Zimbabwe after independence. From less than 240,000 in 1980, the number of tourist arrivals more than doubled in a decade, to more than 550,000 in 1990. The figure exceeded 2 million in 1999, but violent invasions of commercial farms and clashes during elections have caused a dramatic drop in tourist arrivals, as travelers choose to bypass Zimbabwe in favor of its more peaceful neighbors. This has led to lower hotel occupancy rates, the withdrawal of international airlines, and the loss of jobs in the tourism sector.

Tourism earns Zimbabwe around $400 million in foreign currency a year and accounts for approximately 5 percent of the gross domestic product. The Zimbabwe Tourism Authority is working to promote the country as a vacation destination by looking for new markets in Asia and the Middle East and organizing travel fairs. Efforts to revive tourism will have to address the root cause of the slump in the sector—the country's political problems and public violence.

EXTERNAL TRADE

Zimbabwe trades mainly with the United States, the United Kingdom, Germany, and African nations such as Botswana, Malawi, Mozambique, South Africa, and Zambia. Zimbabwe's major exports include tobacco, cotton, manufactured goods, live animals, food products, and fresh cut flowers, while its major imports include petroleum products, machinery and transportation equipment, chemicals, and steel.

Zimbabwe is a member of regional economic organizations such as the Common Market for Eastern and Southern Africa, which aims to remove trade barriers in the region. The country is also one of 14 member states in the Southern African Development Community, which promotes development projects to raise the quality of life of people in the region and improve collaboration among member states.

A woman works on a piece of crochet. Many Zimbabweans earn their living by making and selling handicrafts.

UNEMPLOYMENT

Zimbabwe has a 60 percent unemployment rate. Evidence of the problem can be seen in the city streets, where people with no formal occupation engage in knitting, basket weaving, and other craftwork. The government's failure to redistribute land on a scale big enough to satisfy the large number of poor people living in the rural areas has worsened unemployment. As people leave the countryside to find work in the urban areas, they have to invent ways to support themselves as there are not enough jobs.

ENVIRONMENT

ZIMBABWE'S ENVIRONMENTAL ISSUES are closely connected to its economic issues. Poor industrial management and widespread poverty are big contributors to deforestation, soil erosion, pollution, and loss of wildlife. Other major environmental concerns that Zimbabwe faces include waste disposal and the depletion of natural resources.

WILDLIFE CONSERVATION

Wildlife conservation is one of Zimbabwe's biggest priorities. As in many countries with a rich wildlife and large human population, there is competition for living space in Zimbabwe between people—some 13 million of them—and plants and animals.

Fortunately, wildlife conservation efforts have achieved reasonable success in recognition of the economic value of nature. Zimbabwe's wildlife is a major attraction for tourists, who spend millions of dollars every year in the country's national parks and safari areas. As such, the government has provided substantial support for the upkeep of the country's national parks, which double up as conservation areas and ecotourism destinations. The best-known parks, such as Hwange, Mana Pools, Matusadona, and Victoria Falls, have proper facilities and trained guides to take visitors on walks or canoe rides through natural wildlife habitats while keeping precious species of flora and fauna safe from untrained or uncaring hands.

There are several environmental movements in Zimbabwe that are dedicated to wildlife conservation. The oldest and largest, Wildlife and Environment Zimbabwe, with a global network and nearly 80 years of experience, leads the way in environmental research and national park development, among other things.

Opposite: **Hikers look back for a breathtaking view of the landscape and sky of the Matopo Hills.**

SAVING THE GIANTS

Zimbabwe is home to some mighty creatures. Some of them are native to Zimbabwe; a few live mainly in Zimbabwe; and others are found in other parts of southern Africa as well.

ELEPHANTS Zimbabwe shares with neighboring Botswana the largest population of elephants in Africa. While that may impress visitors, large herds are not easy to support. Full-grown elephants need a lot of food and space. If they become too many for the area they inhabit, these gentle giants look for food elsewhere in the forest or savanna or on farmland, trampling crops and ground vegetation and pushing down trees to eat the fruit and leaves.

Environmentalists have not been able to come to an agreement on the best way to approach this problem. While some advocate leaving the elephant population to a natural cycle of change over time, others support controlled culling—killing a fixed number in reserves every year. The latter option can also generate income from hunters who will pay large sums of money to experience the hunt. On moral grounds, however, culling remains unjustifiable.

ALOE TREES Aloes are hardy plants. They grow on rocky outcrops or cliffs in the drier areas of Zimbabwe. With their succulent leaves, they can survive with very little water. There are hundreds of species, some of which are shrubs and others trees as tall as 16 feet (5 m).

According to the World Conservation Union, southern Africa has the largest concentration of succulent plants in the world, and a fifth of the traded species are threatened. Many aloe species, for example, have medicinal uses that render them vulnerable to commercial exploitation. Possibly around 10 percent of plants in Zimbabwe have been labeled threatened due in part to illegal trade.

There is a society in Zimbabwe that focuses its efforts on widening people's knowledge of aloes, cacti, and other succulent plants through research and walks and on working with similar organizations and the government authorities to conserve such plants. Conservation efforts include growing threatened indigenous species in parks. For example, the Ewanrigg Botanical Garden has a wide range of aloe plants.

Above: **The red flowers of aloe trees in Great Zimbabwe bloom in late winter. The nectar of the flowers attracts birds, especially sunbirds.**

Opposite: **Elephants laze in Hwange National Park.**

THE ENDANGERED AND THE DANGEROUS

According to the World Conservation Union, Africa's black, or hook-lipped, rhino is critically endangered, and the white, or square-lipped, rhino has been classified as near threatened. Zimbabwe is one of the last few places on earth where black and white rhinos survive.

The black rhino is poached for its horn, despite a worldwide ban on trade in the horn. Trade in rhino horn fuels hunting that threatens the black rhino with extinction. The Zimbabwean authorities have resorted to drastic measures in attempts to ensure the future of some 200 black rhinos in the country. One alternative is to shoot rhino poachers; another is to move groups of rhinos to guarded locations. However, extinction remains a real possibility for the black rhino.

In contrast, hippos are common in Zimbabwe. They spend most of the day in swampy areas to keep their skin moist and forage on land in the evening. They can eat around 88 pounds (40 kg) of vegetation a day.

If prevented from returning to the safety of the water after feeding, or if people or other animals intrude upon their territory, hippos can get aggressive, especially if it is the mating season. With their huge bulk, big mouth and teeth, and surprising speed even on land, hippos can be dangerous. There have been reports of hippos attacking people and capsizing canoes.

ENERGY AND THE ENVIRONMENT

Zimbabwe gets almost half of its energy from fossil fuels. Wood is the top fuel in rural areas, while thermal power plants burn coal. The burning of fossil fuels releases pollutants such as carbon monoxide and sulphur dioxide into the air.

Hydroelectric power is a cleaner source of energy. The power of the great Zambezi River has been harnessed by dams and power plants to generate electricity for industrial and residential activity in surrounding areas. However, damming rivers has negative effects on the natural environment. Rivers and their valleys are the habitat of many species of plants and animals that depend on one another and on the flowing water for survival.

The Kariba Dam on the Zambezi between Zimbabwe and Zambia flooded forests in the late 1950s and stranded many animals on small islands. The then Rhodesian government launched Operation Noah to save the animals from drowning as the lake continued to rise. Rangers went out day after day in boats to the islands in Lake Kariba, caught thousands of animals such as antelopes and warthogs in nets, then transported the animals back across the lake. Some of the animals, however, drowned before rescuers could reach them.

Another potential source of energy is sunlight. Solar power is already being used in Zimbabwe, but in very limited ways, such as to heat water in some households. Solar power accounts for a minute proportion of the country's energy. Nevertheless, this clean form of energy has a lot of potential in sunny Zimbabwe. Increasing people's awareness of the usefulness of solar energy and manufacturing solar cells domestically to make them more affordable will help widen residential applications of solar power in Zimbabwe.

Wind is being studied as a potential new energy source in Zimbabwe. Wind power has been used in the country for a long time to drive windmills. The government is looking into developing wind turbine technology that can harness the power of the wind to generate electricity.

AIR POLLUTION

The quality of the air in Zimbabwe, especially in the larger cities, has deteriorated drastically since the 1990s, under the pressure of increasing industrial activity and road traffic. Besides the heavy traffic on Zimbabwean roads, many automobiles in the country are old and emit large amounts of pollutants, including poisonous lead particles and harmful gases such as carbon monoxide.

The big cities are also the most vulnerable to industrial sources of air pollution. In addition to being hubs of industrial activity, they are also population centers, and a lot of their heavy industry, such as chemical manufacturing and oil refining, is located near residential areas.

To reduce the harmful effects of industrial activity and road traffic on the quality of air, the government has enacted new laws that require drivers and manufacturers to equip their automobiles and plants with emission control devices. However, it will take some time to effectively enforce the laws and bring air pollution down to less dangerous levels.

WATER POLLUTION

Water pollution is an especially grievous problem in a country where drought is not an uncommon occurrence. As Zimbabwe urbanizes at a rapid rate, sewage treatment facilities have not developed fast enough to deal with the enormous amounts of domestic and industrial sewage generated by a growing population and manufacturing sector.

Pollutants spread diseases through water and pose a serious health threat. They render river water unsafe for drinking or agriculture. The authorities have considered making companies responsible for effluents that they release into natural waterways. Organizations will eventually be required by law to reduce water consumption to specified levels and to

recycle used water. The government will also monitor the way plants discharge waste to ensure that they do not pollute rivers. Offenders will have to pay for the cost of cleaning up pollution that they cause.

SOLID WASTE MANAGEMENT

To deal with litter in city streets, the Zimbabwean government has considered imposing penalties not only on consumers but on producers as well. The rationale is that if companies are made accountable for litter resulting from the consumption of their products, they will make efforts to reduce the amount of packaging they use.

The urban environment is also at risk due to infrequent garbage collection and poor treatment techniques. Waste left for days attracts disease-carrying pests, while incineration releases harmful gases and particles into the air. Waste management can be improved by hiring private companies to collect garbage and using new technologies to reduce and recycle waste.

Zimbabweans fish with bamboo baskets in the Zambezi. Efforts are being made to protect this important river from pollutants from domestic and industrial areas in the region.

ZIMBABWEANS

THE MAJORITY OF ZIMBABWEANS are Shona, while about 16 percent of the population are Ndebele. The Ndebele are a distinct people whose ancestors were warriors in the Zulu army. The strong ethnic difference between the Shona and the Ndebele has created difficulties for a nation state trying to forge a common identity. During the first few years after independence in 1980, these differences erupted into violent conflict.

The Batonga are a minority group in Zimbabwe whose ethnic origins are uncertain. People of European descent make up the other minority group in the country.

Opposite: **Village women stop for a rest with their bundles.**

Below: **Women and children congregate in a village square for an announcement. Most black Zimbabweans live in rural areas.**

Many of the traditional villages in Zimbabwe are distinguished by clusters of huts made of mud and roofed with grass.

THE SHONA

The ancestors of the Shona people crossed the Zambezi River into what is now Zimbabwe about 1,000 years ago. Today, Shona peoples make up about 80 percent of Zimbabwe's population and can also be found in Botswana, South Africa, Zambia, and Mozambique.

Traditionally, the Shona are farmers and cattle herders. Their rural lifestyle gradually evolved through centuries, but the arrival of the European settlers brought about drastic change. Although most of Zimbabwe's Shona population still live in the countryside, 35 percent now live in cities and towns.

There are important subgroups within the Shona. The dominant subgroups are the Korekore in the north of Zimbabwe, and the Manyika and Ndau in the east. Almost half of the people in southern Zimbabwe who speak the Shona language belong to the Karanga group. They are unique among the Shona, because they are more closely allied with the Ndebele despite their Shona ethnic ancestry.

The Shona make up the majority of the population, and it is hardly surprising that Shona-speaking people occupy many important political positions in Zimbabwe. The country's president, Robert Mugabe, is a Shona, and members of his party are predominantly Shona.

THE NDEBELE

While the Shona came to Zimbabwe looking for land to farm and graze their cattle, the Ndebele came in the mid-19th century as warriors. They eventually settled down as farmers but retained an army that was strong enough to deter the first European settlers from attempting an outright takeover. The very name of the main Ndebele city, Bulawayo, means place of slaughter. This is a reference to the violent struggles that took place among the Ndebele for the right to rule.

The Ndebele today are concentrated in the southwest of Zimbabwe around Bulawayo, where their ancestors first settled. No longer warriors as their ancestors were, the Ndebele nevertheless have a strong sense of their unique history and separate identity.

They express this awareness in one of their proverbs: "*imbokodo kazicholelan*" (im-boh-KOH-doh kahz-ee-koh-LAY-lan), which means that grindstones don't grind for each other. Grindstones have been used since ancient times as a cutting tool to process grains and cereals. The Ndebele philosophy behind the proverb is that each grindstone has a different size, shape, and texture, and one does not put two stones together and expect them to fit perfectly. The implication is that each ethnic group has its own culture and way of life that cannot be easily integrated with that of another ethnic group.

Although they form only 16 percent of the population, the Ndebele people have always played a part in struggles against foreign domination.

INTEGRATING INTO SOCIETY After independence, rivalry between the Ndebele and the Shona was developing into a civil war. The Shona central government sent troops into Ndebele areas to defeat the Ndebele-based opposition party. Terrible war crimes were committed by the government, and many innocent people were killed. In 1988 peace was established, and the Ndebele leader, Joshua Nkomo, who had fled the country, returned as vice-president.

Today, the peace seems to be a secure and permanent one, mainly because the source of conflict had more to do with worries about land resettlement than it did with ethnic differences. Zimbabwe's second university, located in the city of Bulawayo, is predominantly Ndebele, a sign that the country's most important minority group has become an integral part of the mainstream society.

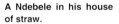

A Ndebele in his house of straw.

THE WHITE MINORITY

Out of Zimbabwe's population of more than 11 million, about 250,000 are not ethnically African. Of these, about 10,000 are Asian, 25,000 of mixed European and African descent, and 80,000 of European descent, most of whom trace their origins to Britain.

In the years of fighting leading up to independence, and immediately after the advent of black-majority rule, an average of 17,000 Europeans fled the country each year. Those who remained in the new state of Zimbabwe were given assurance that their farms and possessions would not be confiscated for at least 10 years, if at all.

A Zimbabwean whiles away her time at a train station reading a newspaper.

The promise was kept. The large and prosperous farms, which covered vast tracts of the country's best land, remained under white ownership. These farms produced around 80 percent of the country's agricultural products, and the white owners maintained a high standard of living.

Relations between blacks and whites in Zimbabwe were better in the years after 1980 than at any other time since the colonists first arrived in 1890. Before 1980 blacks were not able to vote, own the good land that had belonged to their ancestors, or have equal rights in crucial services such as education and health. Few whites had any understanding of the aspirations of the black majority. Many of those who did left the country and sought a life elsewhere.

Relations between whites and blacks reached their lowest point in the years between 1965 and 1980. Once the white-minority government had broken ties with Britain, it felt free to pass laws that openly discriminated against blacks. During that time, the country came to resemble South Africa, with segregation being introduced into areas of public life.

The architecture of the Victoria Falls Hotel is colonial in design. Many of the early buildings in Zimbabwe's towns and cities, especially government buildings, reflect the country's colonial heritage.

THE WHITE POSITION IN THE 1990S Mugabe used the issue of the concentration of wealth in white hands to gain reelection and secure political control. What followed was the seizure of white-owned farms in an atmosphere of violence and intimidation. Racial issues were resurrected as liberation war veterans stated a moral claim to the land of their ancestors.

Today, land ownership remains a divisive issue in Zimbabwe. At the same time, whites and blacks are uniting in opposition to ZANU-PF. The opposition party, MDC, is multiethnic in a way that no other political party has ever been in Zimbabwe.

Many whites who cannot accept the idea of equality are leaving the country, while those who stay have either moderated their views or kept them to themselves.

The legacy of European rule is still apparent in Zimbabwe. Old British cars can be seen on the roads. People drive on the left side of the road. The design of cities such as Bulawayo shows little African influence. Most apparent of all, perhaps, is the widespread use of English.

THE BATONGA

The Batonga are a minority ethnic group in Zimbabwe. Until the 1950s, they lived peacefully in the rural north of Zimbabwe, in a section of the Zambezi valley. The building of the Kariba Dam led to the flooding of their lands, and the group was split into two, one group on the Zimbabwe side, the other on the Zambia side of the river. Batonga families in Zimbabwe had to move farther south in the interior, away from the fertile valley and fresh water of the river.

The Batonga speak a dialect of Ndau, which shares a partial connection to the Shona language, and they have a rich tradition of music and storytelling.

A Batonga home is erected on stilts.

Today, the Batonga are among the most poverty-stricken of all Zimbabweans. They used to make a living by selling their beadwork, but the high cost of materials has made the trade unprofitable. The government is making efforts to improve their standard of living, giving monetary grants to improve sanitation facilities and the water supply. For generations, the white-minority government ignored the Batonga, who had no access to education. This is changing as schools are built in Batonga communities.

LIFESTYLE

MOST ZIMBABWEANS live in the countryside, but the cities continue to attract people in search of material quality of life. In the last 100 years, the more productive land has been farmed by a minority of the people, while the majority struggled to make a living from infertile land. This is still true to an extent, but life for the ethnic Africans, most of whom live in the rural areas, has begun to change as schools and clinics are built in the countryside. Life remains hard, but the future looks more hopeful.

COUNTRYSIDE CONNECTION

Seven out of 10 Zimbabweans work in the countryside. Even in the cities and big towns, many of the inhabitants have close ties with their families in the countryside. Every Friday, bus stations in urban areas are packed with people returning to their villages for the weekend. When they return to the city, they bring back fresh fruit and vegetables to sustain them until the following weekend.

Left: **A boy travels home by bicycle. Most people living in the countryside get around mainly on foot. They may take the bus between villages.**

Opposite: **Two Zimbabwean fishermen mend their nets before setting out for a fresh catch in Lake Kariba.**

With close-spaced homes and large shared areas, village life is community-oriented.

LIFE IN THE COUNTRYSIDE

Life in the countryside is a blend of old and new. Farmers use chemical fertilizers to improve agricultural productivity, yet many cereal crops are still ground manually. Traditional attire has practically disappeared, but ancient rainmaking ceremonies still play an important role.

A characteristic feature of life in the Zimbabwean countryside is people's dependence on walking as the main means of getting around every day. There is always a shop within walking distance, and villagers gather to buy things they need and at the same time chat and exchange news with the shop owner and with other customers. Owning a car is too expensive for most rural farmers. To travel long distances, such as between towns and villages, they hop on a bus.

A typical rural farmer often depends on the sale of his crops to earn money to support the family. However, unlike in the United States, in

COMMUNAL LANDS

The "communal lands" were reserved for the ethnic Africans in Zimbabwe after the first European settlers arrived. The communal lands remain home to large numbers of Zimbabweans today. Before independence, life on the communal lands was extremely harsh. The quality of the soil was generally poor, making it impossible for farmers to increase their harvest without using fertilizers and machinery, which most farmers could not afford.

Since independence, the government has taken measures to help the families living in the communal lands. Pipes have been laid to improve water supply, and grants have been made available to the farmers so that they can buy chemical fertilizers. The increase in the production of corn has been astounding, and the communal lands now produce 12 times more corn than they did before 1980.

There are problems, however. One of the most serious is soil erosion. The communal lands, made up of small family farms, contain more people than do commercial farmlands. Farmers in the communal lands also tend not to manage natural resources as well as large-scale farmers do. The constant need to collect firewood for cooking and timber for building homes and the large herds of cattle that eat the thin grass cover expose the topsoil to the elements of the weather— wind and water. A smaller cattle population might improve the situation, but farmers are reluctant to reduce their stock.

Soil erosion and drought have driven people from the communal lands. The slow pace of land reform adds to the people's dissatisfaction. While the white farmers continue to live on large, productive farmlands, the indigenous peoples wonder if the land that belonged to their ancestors will ever be returned.

Zimbabwe small farmers use a large proportion of their crops to feed the family. They grow corn in their field and take the harvest on foot to the local mill for grinding. That corn serves as the staple food for the household. Firewood for cooking is collected on foot, and people have to walk farther as sources of wood become depleted. Fruit trees and vegetables are also cultivated in the countryside.

A noticeable feature of many village communities is the absence of young men, because they have left the countryside to find work in the cities. They return as often as they can, regarding the village as home, where wife and children are. Many of the young men work on the big commercial farms or travel to towns to work in manufacturing plants. Some go to a different country, such as South Africa, for employment in the gold mines or in factories.

A Zimbabwean woman prepares a meal, just one of her many daily duties.

A WOMAN'S LIFE

Women grow more than half the world's food crops. In Africa, women account for as much as 80 percent of food production. As the men move to the towns and cities for work, more and more women are becoming heads of their households.

Whether or not their husbands are in town, women in the villages have a daunting list of responsibilities, such as collecting firewood and water, cooking, looking after the children, and cleaning the home. They also maintain the vegetable gardens and work in the fields to sow the corn. Fertilizers increase corn yields, but more weeding needs to be done.

When their husbands are away working in the cities, the workload increases for the women in the villages. It then becomes their responsibility to look after the cattle and go to the market to sell the crops.

Women may have to bring their children with them wherever they go. If the child is very young, the mother may carry the child in a sling on her back. Women often carry their goods in a basket on the head. This not only frees their hands to hold their children's hands but also distributes the weight of the basket more evenly throughout the body and reduces the strain on individual muscles.

Despite the tremendous demands that they face every day in the fields and at home, women in the Zimbabwean countryside are not regarded as their husbands' equals. For example, according to tradition only men can inherit or rise to positions of power within a chieftaincy.

RIGHTS FOR WOMEN

They fought alongside men in the country's nationalist struggle, but Zimbabwean women today do not have equal legal status. Among the government's greatest challenges after gaining independence was to promote gender equality. The Legal Age of Majority Act was passed in the early 1980s, finally granting Zimbabwean women the right to vote and many other rights that were previously exclusive to male citizens.

Besides gaining greater access to education and employment, women have also become a force in the political and social spheres, as leaders, activists, or supporters. Opposition parties have won strong support from women voters drawn to the promise of gender equality.

In 1991 Zimbabwe acceded to the United Nations Convention on the Elimination of All Forms of Discrimination against Women. Yet women still face legal discrimination and lack land inheritance rights. It will take time for prejudice to break down and give way to equality between women and men.

Village women weave baskets.

Goats are raised for their meat and milk. A goat or two can supply sufficient milk for a family throughout the year.

A HARD LIFE

In the valleys of the Zimbabwe plateau, life is harsh. The sun glares, and temperatures reach 100°F (38°C) in summer. If there is no rain in winter, the region faces the possibility of drought.

In the valleys far north, the tsetse fly makes it impossible to keep cattle. This means that farmers have to plow the land by hand. There are fewer schools and shops in the region than anywhere else in the country, and the absence of beer halls and markets testifies to a bleak social life for the inhabitants.

A village in a poor northern valley may consist of no more than a few mud-and-pole homes. Villages on the banks of a tributary of the Zambezi River have their own supply of fresh water. Otherwise, a well must be dug, or water must be carried from the nearest source. The woman of the household is up at five in the morning preparing breakfast before leaving for the day's work in the fields. In nearly every family, a father, son, or brother will likely be working outside the village out of economic necessity.

A successful harvest depends on rainfall after December. Without the rain, the cobs of corn and tufts of cotton will not appear. When the rain comes and the crops begin to grow, the fields are constantly raided by animals from the surrounding bushlands. Raids like these can easily destroy the best part of a harvest.

MARRIAGE

In Zimbabwe's rural communities, a young man will offer a large gift to the family of the woman he marries, and she will leave her village to live with him in his. The gift, often in the form of cattle, signifies the man's recognition of the woman's value and the link between their families.

When a woman marries, she adopts her husband's clan name. Clan members claim a common descent through the male line. Although a married woman will use the clan name of her husband, she can never actually become a member of the clan. If the marriage should prove unsuccessful, leading to a divorce, the woman returns to her father's home community and assumes his clan name again.

In the rural communities, it is possible for a man to marry more than one woman, although this is quite rare. When a man dies, his brother may inherit his wife, but she is free to reject a second marriage and go back to her father's village. In the case of divorce or the death of the husband, a woman may be disinherited by her husband's family and have to give up her home, money, and even children.

Many Zimbabwean women are speaking out against polygamy and against customary laws that leave women in a vulnerable position when their husbands die. In the towns and cities, traditional attitudes toward women and marriage are slowly changing. A lot more work needs to be done in the countryside, through education, to erode the assumption of male superiority.

The Ndebele hold initiation ceremonies to mark a person's passage from childhood to adulthood. The Shona mark a person's passage to adulthood by marriage and the birth of the first child. In that sense, marriage is considered natural and inevitable, and an unmarried man or woman can be regarded as an anomaly.

A female police officer and her male colleague prepare to make their rounds. As they venture into the towns and cities in search of work, more women in Zimbabwe are taking jobs once dominated by men.

THE WEDDING GIFT The usual gift to the bride's family in rural marriages is cattle. For the Shona and the Ndebele, cattle are valuable for more than commercial reasons; cattle indicate a family's status and prestige. The larger a family's herd of cattle, the higher its status and the greater its prestige. The gift of cattle in marriage represents the man's commitment to the woman he marries.

BRIDE SERVICE In the poorer areas, a man may be unable to afford to offer cattle in exchange for his bride, or there may be no cattle because of a tsetse fly epidemic. Among the Korekore and the Tande, the husband often makes payment by leaving his village and setting up home in his wife's village, where he does bride service, or *kugarira* (kakh-ah-REE-rah). That means working in the fields of his father-in-law for a period of time, possibly 10 or even 15 years. Having fulfilled the bride service, the husband is allowed to return with his family to his own village. However, he may decide to stay if the family is well-settled. The wife's father may give her family land in the village for their use. The event is marked by various formalities, such as seeking permission from the ancestral spirits of the village for a stranger to join the community.

THE VILLAGE CHIEF

The chief of a rural community holds great social and political power, partly because he claims descent from the original owners of the land. They may be the first people ever to have lived there or the conquerors of the first inhabitants. There is a very strong feeling that the past is connected to the present through the chief, a living descendant of ancestors buried in the land. Significant sites, such as pools and hills, in a village are often named after ancestors, and stories relate how sites are connected with events in the lives of ancestors.

The village chief's role has been changing for a long time. The early European settlers, who held tremendous political power, took away the age-old tradition of distributing land within the chief's territory. In the 1970s, during the struggle for independence, village chiefs who did not cooperate with the European government were replaced by new chiefs who were willing to support the government. Whole villages were resettled in the interest of security.

Contemporary life continues to erode the power of the village chief. The migration of people from the countryside to the cities weakens the chief's influence and power. Modern developments, such as business enterprises and women's cooperatives, do not fit under the traditional authority of the chief.

Traditionally, the village chief is spoken of as the father of his people, and his ancestors are their sekuru *(sah-KOO-roo), or grandfathers.*

73

THE FAMILY

Opposite: Mothers have lunch with their children.

Traditionally, children in Zimbabwe spend more time with their mothers than with their fathers, and the mother is responsible for the education and welfare of her children. One reason for this practice may be that men often have to leave their families to find employment away from home, in which case they may not see their children for months at a time.

The Western notion of a nuclear family, consisting of father, mother, and children, cannot be applied to traditional African society. A typical North American child has a clear sense of the difference between the immediate family structure and the extended family relationships that include uncles and aunts, cousins and grandparents.

The difference is far less obvious in traditional Shona and Ndebele society. Shona and Ndebele in rural areas are largely unfamiliar with the concept of a nuclear family structure. They relate to their relatives as members of one big family, or clan, and it is common for two or more generations to live together. Families are patrilineal, and when a man marries, he brings his wife to live with him in his settlement.

In the past, Zimbabwean men addressed their uncles as fathers and their aunts as mothers. Cousins were either sisters or brothers. However, industrialization and education have broken down extended family relationships. The term cousin is now increasingly used in the Western sense, and the terms uncle and aunt refer to a parent's brother and sister. Nuclear families are the norm in cities, although people still maintain strong links with their relatives.

Despite the process of modernization, the family structure is still a broader-based one than it is in the West. Illegitimacy and orphanhood are not perceived in the same way. An illegitimate or orphaned child would be more likely to find parents within the extended family.

EDUCATION

Christian missionaries played a vital role in establishing schools for the ethnic Africans in Zimbabwe, but they were never able to overcome the institutionalized racism that benefitted the European population at the expense of the Africans. Today around one-third of the adult population has had no formal schooling.

Since 1980 the government has expanded elementary, intermediate, high-school, and college education in the country. Children are entitled to free elementary education, but child labor keeps some of them from completing elementary school. At the high-school level, more trained teachers are needed to meet the demands of the children.

Nevertheless, Zimbabwe has a higher literacy rate than many other African countries. More and more students are finishing high school and qualifying for admission to a university. Unfortunately, the University of Zimbabwe and the University of Science and Technology in Bulawayo are unable to offer places to all who are qualified.

HEALTH

It is thought that as many as 600,000 people in Zimbabwe, or 25 percent of the population, are HIV-positive. AIDS is now the leading cause of death among children under age 5, many of whom are born to HIV-positive mothers. Prominent Zimbabweans in government, entertainment, and sports have died from AIDS.

The government finds it difficult to control the spread of AIDS. People are not educated about the disease and do not think that they can get it. In Zimbabwe AIDS is usually spread through unsafe sex. Hospitals do not have enough beds to treat AIDS patients, and most of them receive inadequate care.

RELIGION

MOST ZIMBABWEANS continue to practice their indigenous religions. They believe that the spirits of their ancestors have an important effect on the present. They seek the advice of ancestral spirits in all areas of life. During the nationalist struggle for independence, it was considered very important to have the support of an ancestral spirit medium who spoke in favor of the rebellion.

Around 25 percent of Zimbabweans are Christians. Christianity was introduced to the country by European missionaries who set up churches and schools for the ethnic Africans. Many of Zimbabwe's political leaders and prominent citizens were brought up as Christians and educated in Christian mission schools.

In recent years, however, the spread of mainstream Christianity in Zimbabwe has declined. What has increased, on the other hand, is the number of independent African churches that combine Christian and traditional indigenous beliefs and practices.

TRADITIONAL RELIGION

Most world religions have some traits in common: a central store of set beliefs and rituals, sacred books, a history of its spread, and a name: Christianity, Islam, Buddhism, Hinduism, and so on. African religious beliefs and practices tend not to have such characteristics and, in the absence of a formal name, are referred to as traditional. The word traditional also points to the fact that such beliefs and practices were in existence long before Christianity or Islam made its impact in Africa.

The main animist cult in Zimbabwe worships a creator god called Mwari (m-WAHR-ee), who is believed to abide in the sky. In times of natural disaster, war, or other social disturbance, contact with Mwari is made through a spirit medium.

Opposite: **A Zimbabwean medicine man. He may be called to cure an illness or exorcise evil spirits.**

A rainmaking spirit medium is much venerated.

POWER OF THE SPIRITS Zimbabweans who practice their indigenous religions believe in powerful ancestral spirits that influence life in ways people cannot control or sometimes even understand. People worship the spirits to appease them and win their favor.

Unlike Mwari, the supreme being, ancestral spirits were once human beings and are thus believed to be more accessible and understandable to the living. The spirits of ancestors are thought to live in a land located under the ground, where they are able to keep watch over the living.

If the spirits are unhappy about something, they send signs of their displeasure. When sickness or a natural calamity occurs, animists may interpret it as a sign that they have offended the spirits. They then go to a shrine, which may be a cave or a tree, to ask the spirits to put things back to normal.

People communicate with ancestral spirits in various ways. They may offer prayers or sacrifices. The most dramatic way is through ritual specialists. They include rainmakers or mediums who can be contacted in order to find the source and the solution of a particular problem. In the case of drought, for example, a Shona rainmaking spirit medium may be contacted to negotiate with the particular spirit that is causing the lack of rain and keeping the crops from growing.

The spirit of a village chief is of special importance. When he dies, he becomes a *mhondoro* (meh-HOHN-doh-roh), which is responsible for the continued fertility of the land in which he was once the guardian. If the will of the *mhondoro* is obeyed, rain will come on time and the crops will grow. If his advice is ignored or a crime is committed, then the rain may be withheld. All the men who work on the land of the *mhondoro* make annual offerings of grain at the first harvest.

PROTECTIVE SPIRITS

Obligations to care for family members are not taken lightly and do not come to an end at the time of death. After death, people are transformed into *midzimu* (mid-ZEE-moo), or ancestors. As *midzimu*, they continue their roles as protective parents, but they wield more power than they ever did when alive. Ancestors perceive what is happening among their living descendants and intervene when they feel it is necessary. They do not act irresponsibly. They might signal to warn of approaching danger or request that a child be named in their memory. One method of showing that they wish to be heard is by causing illness.

A medium often calls on the ancestral spirits for guidance if he is trying to cure an illness.

THE SPIRIT OF NEHANDA

Nehanda was a chief, and so her spirit became a *mhondoro*. In the first rebellion of 1896 against the European settlers, a medium of Nehanda played a major role in leading the uprising. She was eventually captured and hanged, but her defiance became legendary. Tales and songs circulated about her refusal to accept conversion to Christianity and the prophetic words she declared from the scaffold that her bones will rise to defeat the Europeans.

When the second uprising began in 1972, the rebels found that many spirit mediums were once again on their side. *Mhondoro* spirits continued their responsibility to protect the land, and the nationalist demands for returning land from the European minority to the African majority seemed the best way to do this.

After the death of Nehanda's first medium, the *mhondoro* resided with another medium, who was committed to helping the rebels. The government forces were well aware of the danger posed by the spirit mediums and distributed tape recordings and posters of mediums who were against the African nationalists.

Afraid that the government forces might capture and punish the medium of Nehanda, the nationalists persuaded her to cross the Zambezi River and hide in Mozambique. She stayed there until her death in 1973, when she was given a funeral fit for a chief. She was carried to her grave in a white cloth and buried on a wooden platform in the ground, surrounded by a hut that had been built and thatched in a day.

WITCHES

Animists in Zimbabwe believe in witches, or *muroyi* (merh-ROI-ee), who ride about not on broomsticks but on the backs of hyenas. Witches are believed to be responsible for unpleasant deeds such as robbing graves and killing people and turning them into animals. Less dramatically, their presence is felt when a traditional healer or a spirit medium attributes an illness to a spell cast by a witch.

An unfortunate person may become a witch through possession. If this happens, it is passed down from generation to generation, not only from mother to daughter but also from father to son. It is also believed that a witch can be found within one's family.

Witches are so feared that the only effective way to deal with them is to kill them. Beliefs like these can lead to terrible tragedies, especially as possession of a family member is very common. Even today, it is not uncommon to read accounts of deaths occurring in this manner.

The fear of witches is also reflected in rites that take place at some funerals. At the bottom of the grave, a shelf is hollowed out where the body is placed before being covered with a mat and poles. The grave is then filled with stones and earth, and large rocks are piled on the site, forming a large mound.

These rites are carried out in order to make it more difficult for a witch to reach the body. The surrounding area is also carefully swept, so that if a witch attempts to approach the grave, footprints will be left.

A Ndebele medicine man's dwelling.

WITCHCRAFT SUPPRESSION ACT Witchcraft is recognized by Zimbabwean law, although there are problems in defining exactly what constitutes witchcraft. Established at the end of the 19th century and amended in 1989, the Witchcraft Suppression Act declares it illegal to practice witchcraft, or sorcery, or to accuse someone of practicing witchcraft. Offenders may be punished with imprisonment.

In 1997 the Zimbabwe National Traditional Healers Association (ZiNaTHA) proposed a second amendment to the act, to restrict the prohibition of witchcraft to only those acts aimed at causing disease or injury to another person or to an animal. Churches and human rights organizations have generally opposed the proposal.

CHRISTIANITY

Christianity came to Zimbabwe through missionaries in the latter half of the 19th century. Today Christianity has an established role in Zimbabwe as the predominant belief system outside of traditional African religion.

About one quarter of Zimbabwe's population are members of Christian churches. Of that number, more than one-third are members of independent churches. The Roman Catholic and Anglican churches have the largest number of followers. The Methodist and Congregational churches are the two largest Protestant groups. The growth of Christianity in the country has slowed considerably since independence.

The established churches have a mixed relationship with traditional African religion. Some churches have been more receptive than others to the local people's traditional beliefs and customs.

For example, it is not uncommon for the members of certain churches to attend a Sunday morning service after having spent the night at a possession ceremony. Or they might wear a string of black ancestral beads as well as a cross around the neck. In the countryside especially, people would not

have a problem attending Christian church services on a regular basis while continuing to participate in possession ceremonies and make offerings to the local *mhondoro.*

Evangelical churches, on the other hand, are actively opposed to the traditional religions of Zimbabwe. They perceive animist beliefs and practices as ungodly. The drinking of beer, an established part of possession ceremonies, is banned during the services of Evangelical churches in the country. The members of those churches are strictly forbidden from participating in other ancestral rituals as well.

Above: **A Catholic priest celebrates Mass with his congregation in the countryside.**

Opposite: **An Anglican church in Harare.**

Catholic nuns were some of the earliest missionaries in Rhodesia. They spread the faith, tended the sick, and started schools and hospitals.

MISSIONARIES Christian missionaries first arrived in Zimbabwe, then Rhodesia, with Cecil Rhodes at the end of the 19th century. Due to their involvement in politics—for example, it was a missionary who negotiated a treaty for Rhodes tricking the Ndebele leader Lobengula into signing away his people's rights—missionaries were attacked and murdered in the uprising of 1896.

They continued to come after the uprising was put down, and by 1910 there were more African than European Christians in Rhodesia.

Missionaries played a crucial role in educating the Africans. Wherever a church was built, a school followed. Roman Catholic, Anglican, and Methodist missionaries were among those who set up churches and schools in Zimbabwe. Many also established clinics and hospitals, which were often the only places where the ethnic Africans could have access to Western medicine. The missionaries brought many benefits, but their beliefs were often at odds with traditional beliefs.

Missionaries faced a dilemma during the 1970s when the nationalists fought the government. Many supported the nationalists, but many died in the war. While the government blamed the nationalists for the deaths of the missionaries, the nationalists blamed the government.

Today Christian missions continue to flourish in Zimbabwe. Some mission schools are better funded than government schools and provide better education. Many of Zimbabwe's leading citizens, including Robert Mugabe, were educated in mission schools.

THE VAPOSTORI The Apostolic Church strongly opposes ancestral worship. Members of the Apostolic Church, known in Zimbabwe as the Vapostori, spend time exorcising ancestral spirits, or what they consider to be witches.

The Vapostori believe that prayer is the only remedy for disease and illness of both the body and the spirit. They not only oppose traditional medicine but also reject orthodox Western medical practices. This has resulted in distressing cases where children die unnecessarily because their parents refuse to consider using available drugs.

The Vapostori follow strict rules and isolate themselves from society, avoiding state education and law. This has led to a degree of conflict with the government, which wants to see them become more integrated with the rest of society.

LANGUAGE

THE THREE OFFICIAL LANGUAGES in Zimbabwe are Shona, Ndebele, and English. Shona is the mother tongue of nearly seven out of 10 Zimbabweans, while Ndebele is a minority language spoken by about 15 percent of the population. While Shona is spoken across the whole country, Ndebele speakers are concentrated around Bulawayo and the southwest of the country.

English is spoken everywhere. Even in remote rural areas, there is usually someone who can communicate in English. In the larger urban areas, English is widely spoken and is the language of business and government. The middle classes use English partly as a status symbol.

Opposite and below: **English is widely spoken in Zimbabwe and is used for road signs and building names.**

BANTU

Both Shona and Ndebele are classified as Bantu languages. Bantu is the general term for a wide family of languages spoken throughout the southern half of Africa that are believed to have a common origin. The original Bantu language was likely spoken in western Africa, from where it spread south and east. Over thousands of years, Bantu evolved into a large number of languages that are spoken in many areas of Africa. The most widespread Bantu language today is Swahili, spoken in many countries in East Africa.

SHONA

Before the European missionaries arrived toward the end of the 19th century, the Shona language did not exist in the form in which it exists today. Instead, different ethnic groups in Rhodesia spoke different dialects, which made the European missionaries' task of teaching the gospel ever more difficult. The missionaries made a systematic study of the different dialects spoken. The dialects were later brought together and unified under the common label Shona.

The Shona language includes the major dialects Karanga, Korekore, and Zezuru, and their subdialects. Zezuru is spoken in the capital and the surrounding district and is considered very prestigious to use.

People and dialects mix freely in Harare, and an urban form of Shona has evolved. Known as Town Shona or Chishona, it is characterized by a mixture of English and Shona words. Chishona abandons many of the more formal aspects of regular Shona. For example, in Shona, various pronoun forms are used to denote respect when addressing a person who is perceived as a superior. But in Chishona, dialogue takes place without these pronoun forms.

CHILAPALAPA

Chilapalapa (chill-ah-PAHL-ah-pah) is an English-Ndebele pidgin dialect. It developed during the colonial era to facilitate communication between the European farm owners and their African employees. Most of the communication took the form of orders and instructions. This is reflected in the grammar of the language, as the verbs only take the imperative form. For example, there is no verb "to leave," only the imperative form "Leave!"

Chilapalapa is still used in some European households employing African workers, but it is dying out.

NONVERBAL COMMUNICATION

Some of the most appealing forms of nonverbal communication in Zimbabwe deal with etiquette—conventional rules of behavior that govern certain areas of social life.

When accepting a gift, both hands may be held out. This does not suggest that more is expected. Rather, it is an expression of gratitude. Sometimes the person receiving the gift will clap, then hold out both hands, palms up, with fingers slightly crossed to make a kind of shallow spoon. Sometimes only one hand is held out, with the other held across its wrist, reflecting an old warrior's show of friendship.

Handshakes differ among men and women. Men slap their hands loudly, with the flat of one hand in line with the palm of the other hand. Women greet by slapping each other's palms gently. To greet a very important person, men will sit on the ground, clap their hands twice or three times, and wait silently for about 10 seconds, before clapping their hands again.

Formality governs certain occasions, such as a stranger visiting a village where a meeting, or *indaba* (IN-da-bah), is taking place. The newcomer approaches the circle of seated men, squats on its perimeter, and claps his hands gently two or three times.

Nobody says anything until the most senior man in the *indaba* stops talking and allows the others to continue. The visitor waits for a natural break in the conversation, then claps again. If he is welcome, the senior man claps back as an invitation to join the group. Usually, a visitor to a village is greeted by a line of men clapping gently, and women making shrill sounds.

A chicken, a pumpkin, or a handful of eggs may be given as a departing gift. As an expression of affection, the host and neighbors will escort visitors out of the village and accompany them for a mile or so.

Shona children are taught by their mothers to greet their fathers by clapping their hands and shouting "*Kwaziwai baba*" ("Greetings to you, father"). They are also taught a series of greetings for their grandfathers, grandmothers, and male and female neighbors.

A teacher claps her hands to demonstrate to her students the traditional mode of nonverbal communication.

ARTS

WHATEVER ZIMBABWE LACKS in material wealth, it is amply compensated for by a rich artistic tradition. This covers a wide range of art forms, including music, literature, sculpture, and dance.

Zimbabwean art has seen a renaissance since 1980, as political independence has given artists in diverse fields the freedom to express themselves and make themselves known to the country and the world. A *manyawi* (mahn-YAH-wi), the spirit of expression and excitement, is in the air.

Above: **A masked dance accompanied by drums.**

Opposite: **A soapstone sculpture in a Shona handicraft village.**

MUSIC

Zimbabwe's most accomplished and independent art form is music. Zimbabwean music has developed its own identity and style. Some Zimbabwean musicians and bands have become successful enough to tour abroad and entertain people in other nations with their distinctive sounds.

Zimbabwean music defies categorization. It is a blend of African and other cultural influences, fusing rock, jazz, soul, and reggae with the sounds of traditional African instruments. The result, the music of Zimbabwe, has been dubbed Jit Jive.

What distinguishes Zimbabwean music is the use of three particular instruments: drums, a thumb piano, and a marimba. These traditional African instruments were much neglected during the colonial era. Western music followed different rules of harmony from those that governed the music of Africa, and the European colonialists sometimes regarded African music with indifference. Independence returned Zimbabwe's traditional musical instruments to the forefront.

DANCE

Dance permeates all aspects of Zimbabwean life, from religious rituals to political rallies.

In both Western and African culture, dance can function as recreation, entertainment, or a means of courting. Dancing is also appreciated by both cultures as an art form in its own right.

A significant feature of dance in Zimbabwe is its use as a means of expressing spirituality. Traditional African dance reflects a belief in the spirit of the earth as the provider of fertility. African dance usually has a downward orientation—toward the earth—with the feet planted on the ground in firm steps and the knees flexed. Rainmaking ceremonies also involve dancing, and some of the evangelical churches in Zimbabwe incorporate dance into their worship.

THE SHONA PROTEST SONG

The Shona protest song is based on a traditional genre. Protest songs are used to express a variety of emotions, such as sorrow over death or joy of victory in battle. Protest songs are sung by a group; the lead guitarist sings the main storyline, while the other band members sing the chorus. The audience joins in the singing by urging the band to *dzepfunde* (zep-FAHNDE), or go on.

In the years leading up to Zimbabwe's independence, the emergence of protest songs reflected a growing political consciousness among the people. Zimbabwean music of that time reflected revolutionary themes and became a tool to motivate people in the struggle for independence.

God Bless Africa, a song composed in South Africa in 1897 and later translated into the languages of the Shona and Ndebele, became the song of resistance to European rule in Zimbabwe and was sung as a mark of triumph on the day of independence. It has since become the national anthem of South Africa.

SCULPTURE

Zimbabwe's most famous sculptors include Joseph Ndandarika, Sylvester Mubayi, Henry Munyaradzi, and Nicholas Mukomberanwa. Also making an impact in Zimbabwe is the Tengenenge (ten-gen-ENG-ay) school of sculpture. The name comes from a community that specializes in carving serpentine, a dull green rock with markings that resemble those of a serpent's skin. The community was founded in the 1960s by Tom Blomefield, who took up sculpting when his tobacco farm ran into financial difficulties.

A few Zimbabwean sculptors have made it on the international scene, but for many aspiring sculptors the cost of transporting a piece of work to Europe or North America is a big hindrance.

A poster of Chenjerai Hove used to publicize one of his best-known works, *Up in Arms*.

CHENJERAI HOVE was born in 1956. He writes novels and poems in Shona and English. Hove believes that artists have the ability and responsibility to shape their country's hopes and dreams. His English novels, including the award-winning *Bones* (1988), are distinctly Zimbabwean in the traditional Shona sayings and popular myths they contain. Like the works of Charles Mungoshi, Hove's novels explore the threat of urbanization to the rural way of life.

DAMBUDZO MARECHERA was born in 1952. He gained recognition as a talented writer while teaching abroad. When he returned to Zimbabwe, he scoffed at the idea of writing for any political agenda. He felt that he should keep out of politics in order to preserve his artistic integrity. Marechera died in 1987.

One of Marechera's autobiographical works depicts a poet who is rejected by publishers because he will not write nationalistic poems in celebration of the new country. Critics attacked Marechera for not building the African spirit, and they refused to acknowledge him as an African writer. To Marechera, however, his national identity was not as relevant to his sense of self as was his identity as a writer.

DORIS LESSING was born in Persia (now Iran) in 1919 and raised in Rhodesia (now Zimbabwe). She did not have a traditional education but weaned herself on the books of many great writers and became an internationally acclaimed novelist herself. In 1950, newly returned to Britain, Lessing published her first novel, *The Grass Is Singing*, about a European woman in Africa in the context of conflicting relationships between Africans and Europeans there. Many of Lessing's works are set in the world of the European settlers in Africa and explore their relationships with the indigenous peoples.

BRUCE MOORE-KING gave a different perspective of Zimbabwe's struggle for independence in *White Man Black War*, first published in Harare in 1988. As a soldier on the European side in 1970s Zimbabwe, Moore-King experienced first-hand the horrors of war. He described in his book his anger at the violence of which he had been a part:

"I can understand, now, why our countrymen took up arms against us. If these actions and attitudes and forms of selective ignorance displayed by my tribe once caused blood and fire to spread across the land called Rhodesia … Must my tribe reinforce their Creed of racial superiority by denying these, the victors of the war, the basic humaneness of the ability to Anger?"

SHIMMER CHINODYA was born in Zimbabwe in 1957. He has written children's stories, short stories, and novels, including the prize-winning *Harvest of Thorns* (1990), which tells the coming-of-age story of a young man during the unstable period of transition from colonial Rhodesia to independent Zimbabwe. Chinodya addresses such issues as politics and religion in his stories and weaves Shona words into English prose to expose readers to Zimbabwean culture.

LEISURE

THE RHODESIAN GOVERNMENT had a strong interest in sports and invested a substantial amount of money in the construction of sports facilities across the country. However, nearly all sports facilities were reserved strictly for use by the European minority. Today sports provide the major source of leisure activity for many Zimbabweans, participant and spectator alike. The government also continues to support the country's athletes in regional and international games. Quieter forms of leisure include watching television at home or having a few drinks in a beer hall.

Opposite: **A group of Zimbabwean children play a traditional game.**

Below: **A family enjoys a relaxing evening at home in front of the television.**

111

A premier division soccer match is played at the National Sports Stadium.

TEAM SPORTS

Soccer is undoubtedly the most popular team sport in Zimbabwe. Every urban area has its own team competing in a national league. Dynamos, Zimbabwe Saints, Black Rhinos, and Highlanders are the top clubs.

The soccer season runs from February to November, and the league games may attract as many as 40,000 spectators. A very big match in the Super League will attract 60,000. Rural areas have their own teams competing outside the league structure.

Another popular team sport is cricket, and the national cricket squad has played well against other international teams. Rugby is also played in schools and at international competitions.

OTHER SPORTS

Golf and lawn bowling are played across the country, and horse racing is a popular spectator sport. One of the top horse-racing meets, Ascot, is named after a famous track in England.

CONSUMING THE MASS MEDIA

Zimbabweans use the mass media for entertainment as well as for information. There are around 400,000 television sets in the country and more than 100,000 internet users. Radio is the most widespread medium, with more than a million sets distributed in both urban and rural areas.

Zimbabweans may watch television with family at home or with friends in a bar. Viewers watch many programs from the United States and Britain as well as locally produced ones. The Zimbabwe Broadcasting Corporation (ZBC) runs two television channels.

Radio listeners have four nationwide channels to choose from: National FM broadcasts programs in the country's minority languages; Radio Zimbabwe airs programs in Shona and Ndebele for rural audiences; Spot FM is a sports channel; and 3FM plays pop music. At certain times of the day, Zimbabweans can also receive broadcasts from the British Broadcasting Corporation's World Service and the Voice of America.

Reading is very much a part of leisure activity in Zimbabwe's urban areas. The local book industry is publishing a growing number of nonfiction and fiction titles, as well as poetry and drama, in Shona, Ndebele, and English. Some of the major English-language newspapers run online as well as print editions. Dailies include *The Herald* and *The Chronicle*, while weeklies include *The Sunday News* and *The Zimbabwe Independent*. *The Chronicle*, based in Bulawayo, attracted attention in 1988 for its valiant reports on a corruption scandal that implicated a government minister.

Art enthusiasts spend some leisure time in an art class.

GAMES

Rural Zimbabweans have very limited access to shops that sell toys and games. Stores in the cities are far away, and the manufactured toys and games sold there are expensive.

People in the countryside thus invent their own games and toys to entertain themselves. Children may fashion from wire a small model of a car or an airplane, sometimes with movable wheels and a long metal handle that they use to steer the model as they walk.

In the game of *kudoda* (koo-DOH-dah), or *nhodo* (n-HOH-doh), a group of children sit around a scooped-out hollow in the ground about 4 inches (10 cm) in diameter. Players take turns throwing a stone up into the air, picking up smaller stones in the hole, and catching the thrown stone before it falls into the hole. Children in other parts of the world play a similar game called jacks or five stones.

Mahumbwe (mah-HOHM-bay) is a game in which children pretend to take on adult roles, somewhat like playing house. *Mahumbwe* was originally a preparation for one's coming-of-age ceremony. When a new home was set up, a boy and a girl would take charge of it for as long as a month. The boy would go hunting, and the girl would cook. At the end of the period, there would be a special ceremony to mark their coming of age, during which participants of the ceremony would drink beer brewed by the girl.

Ndoma (ne-DOH-mah) is similar to hockey. Both boys and girls can play. Players form two teams and compete to hit a wooden ball over a boundary line.

Adults may play a game called *tsoro* (te-SOH-ROH). Essential to *tsoro* are little stones called *matombo* (mah-TOM-boh) and a wooden board with four rows of 13 or more carved holes. Each player has two rows on

the board and a set of stones. Leaving the last hole in each of the rows empty, the player puts one stone in the second-to-last hole and two in each of the other holes.

The players take turns moving their stones in a counterclockwise direction and taking the opponent's stones that are already in the holes. Other versions of *tsoro* have different numbers of stones and rows, or use the ground instead of a wooden board.

Archeologists have discovered ancient game boards in Zimbabwe's Khami ruins. They believe early peoples, especially royalty, used these boards as divination tools. Other such boards have been excavated from ancient sites in other parts of Africa. The ancient board games live on in the games that people living in those regions now play.

A group of men play *tsoro*. *Tsoro* is an ancient game; *tsoro* boards made from soapstone have been found that date back hundreds of years.

FESTIVALS

IN A COUNTRY where the majority of people still live and work in the countryside, the most important festivals are associated with the land. The coming of the rainy season is crucial for the growing of crops, and rainmaking ceremonies are the most significant events in the rural calendar. Even the preparation of the seeds before the rains come can become a ceremony of its own involving the assistance of a medium.

Opposite: **Zimbabweans celebrate their Independence Day in Harare.**

Below: **A masked dance may be performed to ward off evil, pay homage to ancestral spirits, or give thanks for the harvest.**

MAKING THE SEEDS GROW

Before the rains, the village elders and their wives pay a visit to the resident medium in a special ceremony. The proceedings begin with the medium sharing a specially prepared beer with the male visitors, who sit around the medium in a circle. They eat the evening meal in the light of a small bonfire, after which drum music begins. The women sing a traditional song that is addressed to an ancestral spirit, while others join in the ceremony by dancing and swaying to the rhythm of the drums.

Early the next morning, the villagers congregate, singing and clapping, around the entrance to the medium's home. Dressed in white, the *mhondoro* makes his dramatic appearance from the entrance. There is more singing, followed by a meeting in which various matters of local importance are discussed.

The medium delivers judgment on all matters discussed. He later collects the seeds from the households in the village, sprinkles the seeds with root plants to protect them from pests, and distributes the seeds to the villagers for planting.

Agriculture is one of Zimbabwe's main economic activities. A preoccupation with the land and the growing of crops is an important part of a Zimbabwean's life in the countryside. Important events such as the seed planting ceremony will take place prior to the planting.

RAINMAKING

Like the seed planting ceremony, the rainmaking ceremony is held to ensure a successful harvest, which the villagers depend on for their sustenance. The rainmaking ceremony takes place several days or weeks after the village elders' meeting with the medium.

The season of rainmaking festivals begins around September, when winter comes to an end and spring begins. The summer crops will not flourish without the anticipated rains, and rainmaking festivals may continue to the beginning of the following year. The year 1992 was exceptional, with the drought of the previous year continuing through the first three months of the new year. Rainmaking ceremonies were extended for a longer period than usual that year.

A rainmaking festival is usually prompted by the first sign of the approaching spring rains. Brewing begins, and when the beer is ready, everyone congregates at a location that is recognized for its religious significance. This may be the peak of a hill, the entrance to a cave, or a special tree. Rainmaking is a religious event for the people, who believe that their ancestral spirits influence the annual rains, which in turn affect their welfare. If the rains are late or little, the villagers see it as a sign that the ancestral spirits are unhappy or anxious about something.

The rainmaking festival is associated with darkness. It usually takes place at night and is highlighted by intense singing and dancing. The person who performs the rainmaking ceremony may be the village medium or a more senior medium for whom money would have been collected at the meeting before the rainmaking ceremony. The rainmaker wears black and is believed to have the power to make rain appear by hanging out black cloths.

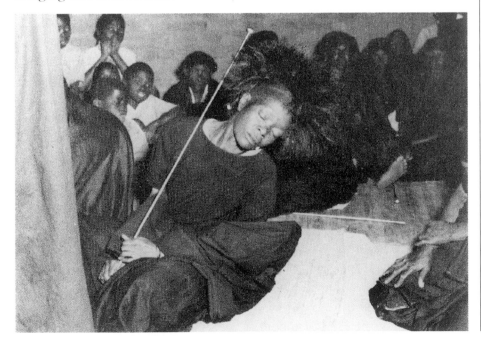

A medium is possessed with her family spirit at a ceremony held to ask for rain from Chaminuka (cham-in-OOK-ah), the greatest tribal spirit.

RELIGIOUS FESTIVALS

The influence of Christianity in Zimbabwe has made Easter and Christmas important parts of the calendar of religious festivals. Even in remote, rural parts of the country, the presence of missions ensures the celebration of special church services to mark the birth, death, and resurrection of Jesus Christ. A dramatic sight in the countryside is the communal prayer gathering of thousands of white-clothed members of the Apostolic Church in a large open area to pray communally.

PUBLIC HOLIDAYS IN ZIMBABWE

January 1	New Year's Day	May 25/26	Africa Day
March/April	Good Friday	August 11	Heroes' Day
	Holy Saturday	August 12	Armed Forces' Day
	Easter Sunday	December 22	Unity Day
	Easter Monday	December 25	Christmas Day
April 18	Independence Day	December 26	Boxing Day
May 1	Worker's Day		

SECULAR FESTIVALS

Zimbabwe celebrates a number of secular festivals that are related to its African identity and nationhood. The country's most important civic festival takes place on April 18—Independence Day.

Zimbabwe's first Independence Day was attended by an array of international figures, including the prime minister of Jamaica and the famous Jamaican musician, Bob Marley. Marley and his band had previously released records that supported the African nationalists who fought the European government in Zimbabwe.

A statue of Scottish explorer David Livingstone stands near Victoria Falls. Livingstone spent 30 years traveling and doing missionary work in southern, central, and eastern Africa.

FOOD

IN ZIMBABWE, food serves a strictly functional purpose. Unlike French or Japanese cuisine, for example, Zimbabwean cooking does not show much concern for the aesthetics of presentation. Nor is there a similar variety of ingredients or flavors.

Nearly a century of colonization has added little to the character of Zimbabwean food. However, the quality of meat in the country is very high, and a Zimbabwean steak is one of the country's tastiest dishes.

Supermarkets in the capital sell canned, bottled, dried, frozen, and other processed and packaged foods that are found in supermarkets in modern cities around the world. However, the traditional Zimbabwean diet is based on corn, vegetables, and some meat.

Left: **Vendors display salted fish in a market in Harare.**

Opposite: **Sacks of grain provided by an Operation Raleigh expedition team in Zimbabwe.**

Corn is sold in markets across Zimbabwe.

CORN

Corn is an important staple in Zimbabwe, being nutritious and readily available. It consists largely of starch, which provides a valuable supply of glucose, but corn is also a source of protein and oil, providing many of the body's essential dietary needs.

Corn is at the heart of traditional Zimbabwean cooking and is used as a core ingredient in many Zimbabwean dishes. Corn is used to make *sadza*, a thick corn porridge that is an essential part of the daily diet. Freshly cooked *sadza* is sold in trains and bus stations, and every rural Zimbabwean knows how to make good *sadza*—by cooking slowly to bring out the taste. Corn is also used to make a thick, white, and rather chewy beer. It is a potent drink that retains the protein of corn.

Corn is so important to Zimbabwe that even in the food crisis of 2002 the government rejected genetically engineered corn from the United States for fear that the corn would contaminate domestic yields.

MEALS AND SNACKS

Apart from *sadza*, a meal usually includes a meat-and-vegetable stew. While the meat is often plain in taste and appearance, the range of vegetables contributes a lot to the taste and color of the meal. Pumpkin, corn-on-the-cob, and butternut squash are common.

People living in the cities have more international food choices. Restaurants offer foreign cuisines, and fast-food outlets serve burgers and french fries.

A rich variety of fruit is readily available. Market stalls are filled with guavas, mangoes, ladyfinger, bananas, papayas, and other kinds of wild fruit that may be less familiar to foreigners.

Zimbabwean snacks are often deep-fried, but there are also baked varieties, such as sweet potato cookies.

Papayas grow on the shore of Lake Kariba.

NDEBELE FOOD

The staple diet of the Ndebele people is based on cereals that are cooked to make a thick porridge known as *isitshwala* (is-eet-KWA-lah). *Isitshwala* is eaten with milk and vegetables.

The Ndebele have a long tradition of hunting, going back to the early days before they settled as farmers. They used dogs to trace the scent of their quarry and *knobkerrie* (k-NOB-ker-ree) clubs to deliver the killing blow. According to tradition, the best meat from a hunting expedition was claimed by the hunter whose *knobkerrie* or spear killed the animal.

Eating cured meat is another tradition in Ndebele culture, although it is no longer as common as it once was. The meat is flavored with salt and herbs, and sometimes left to dry in the sun before being eaten.

BARBECUES AND BREAD

Barbecues, or *braaivleis* (brah-IV-lees), are common in Zimbabwe. The cooked steak is often eaten with *boerewors* (BOH-vorz), or spicy sausage, and a bowl of *sadza. Sosaties* (soh-SAH-teez) are pieces of mutton that have been seasoned overnight with curry sauce and tamarind, and then barbecued or fried.

Rural Zimbabweans may barbecue inside the home, which is often a simple structure of upright poles plastered with clay and topped with a conical roof of thatched grass. The kitchen section may consist of three stones around a fire to support the cooking pots. With no windows or chimney, the smoke from the fire is left to find its way out through gaps between the roof and the upper edge of the walls.

Bread was traditionally baked thick and almost black, with all the natural fiber retained. Today, most Zimbabweans eat white bread.

FOOD CRISES

In a country that is so dependent on agriculture, prolonged drought has devastating consequences. With drastically reduced crop yields, people cannot feed themselves or their animals, and even staple foods such as corn have to be imported.

Millions of Zimbabwean men, women, and children suffered from hunger and malnutrition during the food crisis in 2002. Monthly corn handouts from the government and relief organizations could not cope with the dietary demands of the large families in affected villages. Even wild fruit and water were in short supply. The country went from being a grain exporter to importing staple foods, which still fell far short of consumption needs. The last drought that led to such a severe crisis occurred a decade earlier, in 1992.

Drought in 2002 triggered a web of related problems, the effects of which worsened in 2003. Crop shortages resulted in seed shortages. Shortages of seeds and fertilizers resulted in less planting and poorer harvests. Poor harvests, exacerbated by a lack of rainfall, resulted in a shortage of food crops, which in turn resulted in skyrocketing prices, which made basic foodstuffs very expensive. Bread prices, for example, soared as Zimbabweans turned to bread as an alternative to cornmeal.

In addition to natural causes, human factors contributed to reduced crop yields and further complicated the food crisis of 2002. Violent takeovers of commercial farms were one of the major causes of the country's reduced agricultural productivity.

Zimbabweans hit by the drought of 2002 receive cornmeal from World Vision International and the World Food Program.

SADZA (CORN PORRIDGE)

This Zimbabwean staple may be eaten alone or with a stew or salad. This recipe makes four servings of pumpkin-and-peanut butter-flavored cornmeal.

2 cups water
1 cup cornmeal
½ pound cooked and mashed pumpkin
2 tablespoons peanut butter
½ teaspoon sugar

In a bowl, add half a cup of water to the cornmeal. Mix well. In a deep saucepan, bring the remaining water to the boil. Add the cornmeal paste, one spoon at a time, stirring constantly to prevent lumps from forming, until the mixture becomes a smooth porridge. Stir in the mashed pumpkin, one spoon at a time. Add the peanut butter and sugar. Mix well. Cover, and cook over low heat for one or two minutes. Serve warm as a side dish.

SWEET POTATO COOKIES

Sweet potato adds a unique color and flavor to this snack. This recipe makes 50 to 60 cookies.

2½ cups all-purpose flour
1½ teaspoons baking powder
½ teaspoon baking soda
¼ teaspoon salt
½ cup margarine
¼ cup sugar

1 tablespoon grated lemon peel
½ teaspoon ground nutmeg
¼ cup honey
1 egg, lightly beaten
1 cup peeled, grated sweet potato

Preheat oven to 375°F (190°C). Sift the flour, baking powder, baking soda, and salt in a mixing bowl, and set aside. Cream the margarine and sugar in a separate mixing bowl. Add the lemon peel, nutmeg, honey, and egg, and mix well. Then add the sweet potato, and mix well. Blend in the sifted ingredients to make a dough. Use a teaspoon to shape balls of the dough. Arrange the dough balls at least ½ inch (1.3 cm) apart on a cookie sheet, and bake for 25 minutes, or until golden brown. Then remove the cookies from the sheet and put them on a rack to cool.

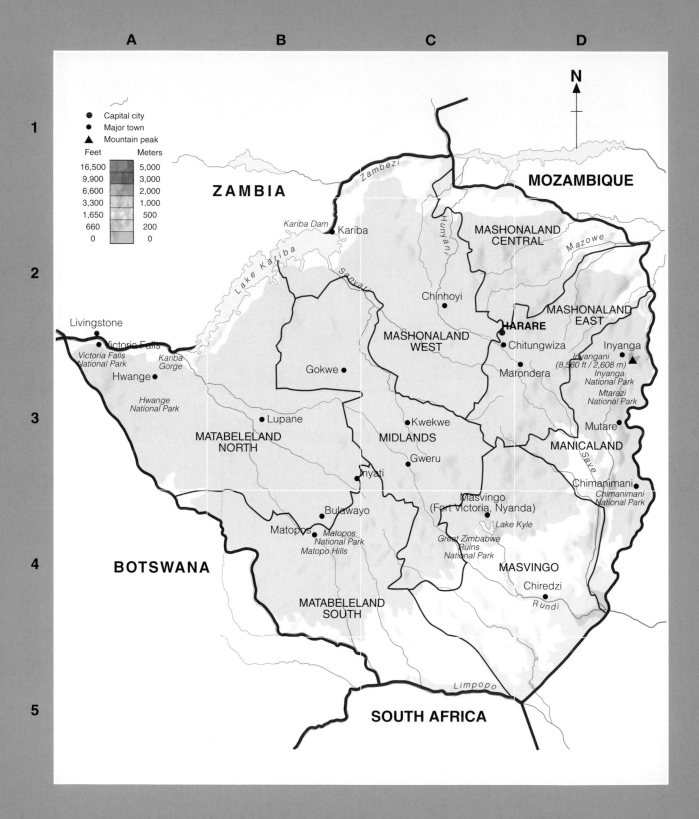

MAP OF ZIMBABWE

TIME LINE

IN ZIMBABWE	IN THE WORLD

8000 B.C.
San hunter-gatherers populate the area.

753 B.C.
Rome is founded.

116–17 B.C.
The Roman Empire reaches its greatest extent, under Emperor Trajan (98–17).

A.D. 300
Bantu peoples arrive.

A.D. 500
Shona peoples grow sorghum and millet, and raise cattle.

A.D. 600
Height of Mayan civilization

1000
The Chinese perfect gunpowder and begin to use it in warfare.

1150–1450
The stone city of Great Zimbabwe is built.

1512
The Portuguese arrive, marking the start of European interest in the area.

1530
Beginning of trans-Atlantic slave trade organized by the Portuguese in Africa.

1558–1603
Reign of Elizabeth I of England

1620
Pilgrims sail the *Mayflower* to America.

1776
U.S. Declaration of Independence

1789–1799
The French Revolution

1840
Mzilikazi, a former warrior in Shaka Zulu's army, establishes a Ndebele community.

1861
The U.S. Civil War begins.

1869
The Suez Canal is opened.

1870
Lobengula becomes king of the Ndebele.

1890
Cecil Rhodes, with 200 gold prospectors and 500 policemen, establishes Fort Victoria.

1895
The Ndebele are defeated.

1896
The First Chimurenga

1914
World War I begins.

1923
Rhodesia becomes Southern Rhodesia.

IN ZIMBABWE	IN THE WORLD
	1939 World War II begins.
	1945 The United States drops atomic bombs on Hiroshima and Nagasaki.
	1949 The North Atlantic Treaty Organization (NATO) is formed.
1957 The African National Congress (ANC) is formed.	**1957** The Russians launch Sputnik.
1961 The Zimbabwe African National Union (ZANU) is formed.	
1965 Prime minister Ian Douglas Smith signs a Unilateral Declaration of Independence.	**1966–1969** The Chinese Cultural Revolution
1972 The Second Chimurenga	
1980 Robert Mugabe is elected prime minister of independent Zimbabwe.	**1986** Nuclear power disaster at Chernobyl in Ukraine
1987 Mugabe becomes president.	
1989 ZANU and ZAPU merge to form the Zimbabwe African National Union Patriotic Front (ZANU-PF).	**1991** Break-up of the Soviet Union
1992 Severe drought leads to a food crisis.	**1997** Hong Kong is returned to China.
1998 Violent seizure of European farms begins.	
1999 The Movement for Democratic Change (MDC) opposition party is formed.	**2001** Terrorists crash planes in New York, Washington, D.C., and Pennsylvania.
2002–03 Food crisis; Mugabe wins presidential elections amid accusations of vote rigging.	**2003** War in Iraq